Computers
and the Cosmos

TIME
LIFE ®

Other Publications:
THE TIME-LIFE GARDENER'S GUIDE
MYSTERIES OF THE UNKNOWN
TIME FRAME
FIX IT YOURSELF
FITNESS, HEALTH & NUTRITION
SUCCESSFUL PARENTING
HEALTHY HOME COOKING
LIBRARY OF NATIONS
THE ENCHANTED WORLD
THE KODAK LIBRARY OF CREATIVE PHOTOGRAPHY
GREAT MEALS IN MINUTES
THE CIVIL WAR
PLANET EARTH
COLLECTOR'S LIBRARY OF THE CIVIL WAR
THE EPIC OF FLIGHT
THE GOOD COOK
WORLD WAR II
HOME REPAIR AND IMPROVEMENT
THE OLD WEST

This volume is one of a series that examines
various aspects of computer technology
and the role computers play in modern life.

UNDERSTANDING COMPUTERS

Computers and the Cosmos

BY THE EDITORS OF TIME-LIFE BOOKS

TIME-LIFE BOOKS, ALEXANDRIA, VIRGINIA

Contents

The Radiant Universe

As recently as the 1950s, the sole source of information about an object in space was the light it radiated. Today, astronomers study not just light but virtually all types of radiation emitted by celestial bodies, from X rays to radio waves.

Every object in the universe with a temperature above absolute zero gives off electromagnetic energy consisting of electric and magnetic fields that vary at a regular rate, generally expressed as a wavelength. Hot sources radiate at shorter wavelengths than cooler ones. For example, dark, cool clouds of gases emit radio signals having wavelengths of more than ten centimeters, thousands of times longer than a star's visible light or ultraviolet and infrared wavelengths. Superheated gases hurtling away from an exploding star release X rays whose wavelengths may be only a millionth of a centimeter. Many objects in the sky, being cooler in some spots than in others, produce emissions of more than one kind (left).

The gathering and analysis of all this electromagnetic information is utterly dependent on computers. At the world's great observatories, photographing the sky—long a prime activity of astronomers—has given way to a new kind of imaging. Radiation is channeled to an electronic detector that creates a digital picture to be displayed on a computer monitor or stored on magnetic tapes or disks for future reference. Computers can process the data in a variety of ways. Perhaps the most spectacular is false-color processing, a technique that permits the addition of colors to images. The varied hues help astronomers see patterns in the radiation they collect—or, as in the image at left, create a composite view containing a sweep of wavelengths from very long to very short (left).

Temperature variations within the gaseous remains of a supernova are highlighted in this false-color composite image of Cassiopeia A, a massive star that exploded more than 300 years ago. The green sections, representing X-ray emissions, reveal a superhot shell of gas that was flung out from the point of explosion at a speed of 20 million miles per hour. At the top of the image, reddish yellow regions produced by an optical telescope show cooler pockets of gas, which originated deep within the deceased star. Electrons spiraling around the shell's magnetic field at nearly the speed of light are responsible for Cassiopeia A's radio emissions, coded here in blue.

The Spawning Grounds of Stars

The space between stars, though dark and very cold, is not a void; hydrogen gas and fine grains of dust are everywhere. In places, the dust and gas have gathered into immense clouds, known as nebulae, that may span tens of light-years. (A light-year is the distance that electromagnetic radiation travels in a year—about six trillion miles.)

Nebulae such as the huge Carina nebula at left intrigue astronomers because such clouds are stellar nurseries. When the dust and gas reach a critical density, gravity pulls the matter together at an ever-increasing rate. As the cloud is compressed, its temperature rises until—at 20 million degrees Fahrenheit—nuclear reactions begin and a new star bursts into radiance.

During the past two million years, much of the matter making up the Carina nebula has coalesced in this manner. Two of the cloud's clusters, called Trumpler 14 and Trumpler 16, contain some of the most massive stars present in our galactic neighborhood.

◄ A box superimposed on a photograph of the Carina nebula *(left)* contains the star clusters Trumpler 14 and Trumpler 16, both surrounded by glowing dust that obscures individual stars. Within Trumpler 14, however, burns the star HD 93129A, which shines with the intensity of five million suns. Eta Carinae, the centerpiece of Trumpler 16, has 120 times the mass of the Sun.

ETA CARINAE

20 ARC MINS

An infrared image of Trumpler 16 pierces the interstellar dust to reveal Eta Carinae as a spot of red, the false color assigned to the most intense areas of infrared radiation. Other colors show the infrared glow of the dust cloud as the level of energy declines with increasing distance from the star. Trumpler 14 does not appear; the cluster emits infrared radiation at a different wavelength from the one used to make this image.

The dark blue area corresponds to the luminous corner within the box on the opposite page. Trumpler 16 is represented by two strong X-ray emitters that appear as light spots at the center of the picture; Eta Carinae is the one on the right. HD 93129A is the light spot above and to the right of Eta Carinae. The dark lines passing through the medium blue area are shadows of the telescope supports.

Shapes
of Galaxies

Mutual gravitational attraction holds prodigious numbers of stars together in the assemblages called galaxies. The Sun belongs to the Milky Way galaxy, a congregation of 200 billion stars arranged in a central bulge and a surrounding disk patterned by spiral arms. As with most spiral galaxies, the central bulge is composed of older, reddish stars, while the dusty, gas-rich arms are studded with new stars that burn a bright blue. But not all galaxies are spirals. Some, called ellipticals, are huge balls of old stars. Others, known as irregulars, assume a wide range of fantastic forms—probably the consequence of collisions between spirals.

The images on these two pages, taken at four different bands in the spectrum, reveal different facets of the spiral galaxy M51, nicknamed the Whirlpool, and its smaller galactic companion NGC 5195.

◄ The visible-light image at left shows M51 joined to its diminutive companion by a tenuous ribbon of matter. M51's spiral arms—which span 65,000 light-years—have a blue glow, indicating the presence of hot young stars. M51 has an unusually brilliant center.

A radio image of M51 (above) dispels the glow of illuminated dust and reveals the spiral arms to be narrow and well defined. False color has been added to this image to code the intensity of radio emissions—blue for the least intense, through green, yellow, and red for the most intense.

The distribution of young stars in the two galaxies is emphasized by this ultraviolet image, in which intensity increases from blue through yellow, green, and red. The outskirts of the Whirlpool are devoid of new, ultraviolet-emitting stars, as is its companion galaxy. The most active regions of star formation, shown in red, correspond to the most luminous parts of the optical image.

The infrared image above underscores the distribution of older stars in the two galaxies. Because they are cooler than new stars, they radiate strongly in the infrared region of the electromagnetic spectrum. At these wavelengths, the companion galaxy, with its preponderance of old stars, rivals the brightness of its neighbor.

Probing the Mysterious Quasar

First detected in 1963, quasars are believed to be the most radiant and among the most distant objects in the universe. The name quasar is a contraction of quasi-stellar object, a title chosen because, to their discoverers, quasars seemed like ordinary stars when viewed through optical telescopes, yet they displayed unusual characteristics when observed in the X-ray, ultraviolet, and radio bands. A quasar often has two radio-emitting jets of gas that blast out from either side of its core. In addition, the strength of a quasar's radiation may vary within a period of a few days. To astronomers, such rapid fluctuations indicate that quasars are quite small—even though their energy output is far greater than that of ordinary galaxies. Many astronomers believe that their power plant is a very massive black hole that spews radiation as it gobbles dust and gas. The quasar in these photographs, named 3C273, lies more than two billion light-years from Earth.

◄ In the image at left, 3C273 appears smeared and artificially large, the result of the long exposure necessary to reveal the faint trace of a gas jet streaming out of the object. A second jet, unseen, is believed to issue from the far side of the quasar.

A view of 3C273's radio emissions, taken by the Merlin telescope in England, shows a gas jet as a brilliant spurt that extends 1.2 million light-years from the quasar. In this portion of the electromagnetic spectrum, both the quasar and the jet are powerful sources, each radiating a million times more radio energy than the entire Milky Way galaxy.

The quasar 3C273 appears as a white spot surrounded by a halo in this X-ray photograph from NASA's High Energy Astronomy Observatory 2 (page 72). The halo is a phantom created by the X-ray telescope used to make the image, while the blue and white "snow" results from random background noise in the X-ray region of the spectrum.

A New Age
of Seeing

In the late 1880s, Edward Charles Pickering, director of the Harvard College Observatory, made a decision that foreshadowed the future of astronomy. To sort through and analyze a torrent of data pouring in through the observatory's telescopes near the university—and about to surge out of control with the opening of a new field station in Arequipa, Peru—he assembled a phalanx of talented graduates of Radcliffe, Wellesley, and other women's schools in the Boston-Cambridge area. Prejudices of the day prevented females from becoming astronomers, but they could and did work for Pickering as "women computers," as they were known at Harvard. They were the opening gambit in what would become, a hundred years later, astronomy's utter dependence on electronic computers.

Pickering's computers played a vital role in the development of modern astronomy. The flow of information from Harvard's observatories had reached flood stage because of a leap in technology fully equal to the introduction of the telescope two and a half centuries earlier—the invention of the photographic plate. Though photographic emulsions of the late nineteenth century were no more sensitive than the human eye, they had the great advantage of being able to record faint objects by accumulating light for hours at a time. The eye, by contrast, cannot store light for more than a few hundredths of a second.

This great advance made it possible for astronomers to look deeper into the universe, to see stars and other objects never before observed. Had it not been for the ability of Pickering's human computers to analyze the immense volume of data contained on Harvard's photographic plates, the advantages of this new technology would have been largely wasted. The forty-five women employed by the observatory during Pickering's years as director recorded the positions of tens of thousands of stars and classified them according to brightness and the characteristics of the light they emitted. It is fair to say that the star classifications performed at Harvard laid the foundations for the discovery that stars blaze with energy produced by thermonuclear fusion—squeezing two atoms of hydrogen together to make one of helium—and evolve through a sequence of well-defined phases in the course of their existence. The efforts of one of the women, Henrietta Leavitt, also led to the discovery that the Solar System is part of a galaxy containing hundreds of billions of stars in a spinning disk with a diameter of a hundred thousand light years.

By 1925, Edwin Hubble, an astronomer on the faculty of the California Institute of Technology, had confirmed the existence of countless other galaxies fully as large and magnificent as the Milky Way. This discovery was made possible by another technological advance, a powerful new telescope installed on Mount Wilson in southern California. Hubble and his colleagues could find no limits to the realm of galaxies. It seemed that with every hour's exposure of their photographic plates, additional faint and wispy smudges appeared, unveiling distant tracts of space never before detected. Hubble summed up the situation eloquently in 1936: "With increasing distance, our knowledge fades and fades rapidly. Eventually we reach the dim boundary—the utmost limits of our telescopes. There we measure shadows, and we search among ghostly errors of measurement for landmarks that are scarcely more substantial."

Hubble was the father of a branch of astronomy called observational cosmology, the study of the largest structures and patterns in the universe. The goal of cosmologists is to understand how these structures, which may be mosaics of tens of thousands of galaxies and may span hundreds of millions of light-years, came into existence and evolved to their present state. With this knowledge, cosmologists hope to determine whether the universe is finite or infinite.

PEERING INTO THE PAST

These are not modest goals, and modest scientific instruments will not do the job. Light that reaches the Earth from the most distant galaxies began its journey ten or more billion years ago. Looking at those galaxies with a telescope is like looking backward through time to see what the universe was like when it was young. Light that has traveled such distances is exceedingly faint—a ten-watt light bulb on the Moon would produce a brighter glow. For this reason, cosmologists yearn continually for improved telescopes—instruments with greater sensitivity to detect fainter objects and with greater acuity to focus the objects more sharply.

Nor are cosmologists alone in their desire for better tools. Astronomers of every stripe need them in the search for evidence to explain such diverse phenomena as comets, the formation of stars, supernova explosions that end the lives of the largest stars, and the mysterious envelopes of invisible, dark matter that surround most galaxies.

As today's astronomers—women now, as well as men—expand the boundaries of the known universe, they confront a deluge of data that would have astounded Edward Pickering and his cohort of analysts. In consequence, high-speed electronic computers have become essential to the study of the heavens. Though not as intelligent as the Harvard women, these machines perform calculations much more quickly and with far greater accuracy and reliability. These qualities are now crucial in every aspect of astronomy. In particular, computers have made possible the construction of an innovative generation of telescopes and promoted the use of sensitive microelectronic detectors in place of photographic plates. These new detectors generate enormous amounts of raw data— the equivalent of a 300-page book in the course of a five-minute observation. Powerful computers, such as Digital Equipment Corporation's VAX, have become essential to refining, storing, and analyzing this information.

Beyond the realm of visible light, computers have made possible instruments sensitive to other kinds of radiation—radio waves and microwaves, infrared and ultraviolet light, as well as X rays and gamma rays. These tools have produced most of the significant discoveries about the universe made since the mid-1960s: enigmatic quasars, pale blue objects far off in space emitting torrents of radio waves and X rays; mind-boggling black holes, possessing gravitational fields so strong that even light cannot escape; and the unrelieved hiss of a cosmic background radiation, thought to be a relic of the Big Bang in which the universe was conceived.

In addition to expanding the choice of tools used to examine the skies, computers provide a new approach to the complex hypothetical questions raised by the observations of astronomers. Working in programmers' code, theorists produce for computers digital mock-ups of stars, galaxies, even the entire universe. Programmed with laws of physics relating mass, gravity, and motion, for example, the computer charts the evolution of the model system. In other words, the computer has become a laboratory in which to re-create cosmic history.

Without computers, such models would be no more than a gleam in a cosmologist's eye. X rays, as far as they concern the stars, would have contributed little to mankind's knowledge of the heavens. Even the astronomer's oldest window to the cosmos, the telescope, would years ago have reached its limits in the huge Mount Palomar telescope in California, begun by George Ellery Hale in the 1930s and completed after his death in 1949.

REFLECTIONS OF THE UNIVERSE

The heart of the problem lies at the heart of the telescope—its curved mirror, a shallow parabola of glass that focuses starlight onto a photographic plate or some other sensor. The basic plan for building a more powerful telescope is simple: Make a larger mirror. In essence, the amount of light that a telescope captures—and hence its ability to see faint galaxies—increases with the size of the mirror. The difficulty lies in fabricating large mirrors, as Hale and his associates at the California Institute of Technology learned when they set about building a whopper—a mirror 200 inches across. Twice the diameter of its nearest rival, the reflector in the telescope used by Edwin Hubble on Mount Wilson, the Palomar mirror weighed nearly fifteen tons. The first attempt to cast a disk of glass for the reflector mirror failed. The second casting took ten months to cool. Grinding away the surface to form a parabolic depression and polishing the surface afterward required several years.

Shaping the mirror, according to some engineers, was the easy part. There remained the herculean task of supporting the huge reflector so that it would not sag, warp, or crack as temperatures changed inside the observatory and as the telescope turned to track stars across the sky. This problem was solved with a mirror-support system that weighed more than 500 tons and a mounting and maneuvering system estimated to contain 36,000 moving parts. Small wonder that the conventional wisdom among astronomers in the decades that followed was that 200 inches represented the largest practical reflector for optical telescopes. This view was reinforced by the experiences of astronomers in the Soviet Union. A 236-inch telescope built by Soviet technicians in the Caucasus during the 1970s was plagued with problems from the beginning and has yet to meet expectations.

In the late 1960s, however, winds of change had already begun to blow. Frank Low, of the University of Arizona, had a peculiar problem. He had developed promising new techniques for studying the infrared light of faint stars and galaxies, but for reasons that he could not explain, his detectors seemed to work best on modest-size telescopes and less well on the very large ones needed to see the most distant objects. To solve the problem, Low decided to increase telescope sensitivity for his experiments by designing an instrument that utilized several small reflectors rather than one giant mirror.

For the idea of a many-mirrored telescope, Low was indebted to the work of Pierre Connes, an inventive astronomer at Meudon Observatory in France. Connes had constructed a prototype telescope having a mirror divided into segments. When properly aligned, they reflected light to a single focus, just as a one-piece parabolic telescope mirror does.

Low discussed his idea for adapting Connes's experiment to several relatively small mirrors with colleagues Gerard Kuiper and Aden Meinel, who were likewise intrigued by the concept. The three men began to mull over alternative approaches to the design of large telescopes. As it happened, Meinel was then working as a consultant to the U.S. Air Force, developing lightweight telescopes for spy satellites, and he knew of some surplus air force parabolic mirrors that could be acquired cheaply.

Within a year, Meinel and Low came up with a preliminary design for a multiple-mirror telescope that, unlike the segmented mirror of the Connes telescope, would combine distinct images from several mirrors to form a single

Project managers at Corning Glass Works inspect the casting for the Hale telescope's 200-inch mirror, examining it for evidence of internal strains before shipping it from New York to California in 1935. As a weight-saving measure, the back of the reflector was molded with a honeycomb structure. Even so, the mirror, made of Pyrex to resist expansion and contraction with changes in temperature, weighed fifteen tons. Casting and cooling the glass took three years; polishing it consumed nine years more.

image. Similar ideas had been proposed earlier, but none had been pursued because of the complexities of combining the separate images. By the late 1960s, however, advances in computer technology spurred by the United States space program had made the plan seem feasible. The University of Arizona team was ready to go. All they needed was money to pay for building the telescope, and a mountain to put it on.

A PEAK FOR THE MMT

Meanwhile, Fred Whipple, director of the Smithsonian Astrophysical Observatory in Cambridge, Massachusetts, had a superb site for a telescope on Mount Hopkins in southern Arizona and had himself been studying alternative telescope designs. When he learned of the efforts of the Arizona group, he proposed a collaboration. The Smithsonian Institution would, with the help of funds from Congress, furnish the site, the building, and the telescope mount, which would support the instrument and enable it to track stars with precision. The University of Arizona, with funding from the Arizona legislature, would be responsible for the optics and the computerized system for aiming the telescope and combining the multiple images.

The Multiple-Mirror Telescope, or MMT, as it became officially known when it was dedicated in 1979, represented the first significant innovation in telescope design since the 200-inch masterpiece on Mount Palomar was put into service thirty years earlier. The new instrument consisted of six separate telescope systems—each with a six-foot primary mirror to capture incoming light, and two smaller reflectors, called secondary and tertiary mirrors, to direct the light into a six-sided pyramid of solid glass. There the beams from the six telescopes were combined into a single image.

"The real challenge," explained Michael Reed of the University of Arizona, who helped develop the system for keeping the telescopes aligned, "was to devise a way for maintaining a stable image each time the MMT changed position or when temperature variations in the observing chamber caused any one of the telescopes to point in a slightly different direction." The mirrors for the six telescopes would have to be aligned with great precision, or their separate images would not come together at a point, and the result would be a useless blur. A computerized system was conceived that would constantly monitor the mirror positions and correct the alignment as needed. In the early days of the development effort, various approaches to this scheme were tried. One involved making the mirrors align on a laser beam fired through the telescope. This approach actually worked, but it had a serious flaw. In the wilds of the Santa Rita Mountains, where the MMT resides, moths and other bugs were attracted to the laser light. And each time one of the creatures flew into the beam, it threw the sensitive alignment controls out of whack.

The eventual solution lay in using the stars themselves to align the six mirrors. A computer first determines very accurately where the target star falls on each telescope's primary mirror. A computer program then instructs a group of small motors to tilt the secondary mirrors (the tertiary mirrors remain stationary) so that all of the reflected images lie directly on top of one another when they arrive at the prism. This process must be performed repeatedly and completed in a fraction of a second *(pages 43-51)*.

Automatic Astronomy

Much astronomical work focuses not on the distant mysteries of the universe but on stellar phenomena close to home. Among the most interesting objects in our cosmic neighborhood are variable stars, so named because their brightness fluctuates. Such firefly behavior can result from expansion and contraction of the star, eclipses by a stellar companion, or massive storms on the star's surface. Since many such stars are located in our galactic vicinity, they can be studied with a telescope of modest sensitivity; a light-gathering mirror as small as ten inches in diameter is sufficient. But they must be observed often to establish the schedule of the variations.

Such a regimen would be a burden on astronomers were it not for the Automatic Photoelectric Telescope (APT) Service in Phoenix—a project managed jointly by the Smithsonian

Telescopes point skyward from the top floor of the APT observatory. Protected by a slide-away roof during the day, the telescopes are automatically uncovered each evening after sunset on instructions from the site computer. Should rain, snow, or an overcast develop, an automated weather station at the observatory informs the site computer, which promptly closes the roof to protect the instruments from the elements. In addition to telescopes and computers, there are workshops at the site for calibrating instruments, and sleeping quarters for the occasional overnight visitor.

Weather Station

Telescope

Slideaway Roof

Institution and the Fairborn Observatory. Established in 1985, APT permits astronomers to do their research wherever and whenever they please.

An experiment submitted to APT is assigned to one of several telescopes at the project's unmanned station atop Mount Hopkins near Tucson, Arizona *(below)*. Once the assignment is made, all the work is handled by a linked group of computers at the observatory—a kind of general manager called the site computer, plus separate computers for each telescope. The telescope computers automatically select which star to observe, aim the telescope at it, measure its brightness, and record the data on storage disks. Every night, each telescope may spend less than ten minutes on as many as eighty experiments.

Whenever the storage disks become full—typically after about a month of observation—an APT technician visits the mountaintop and brings back the information to Phoenix. There, the results of each experiment are transferred to floppy disks, which are then mailed to the astronomers who commissioned the experiment.

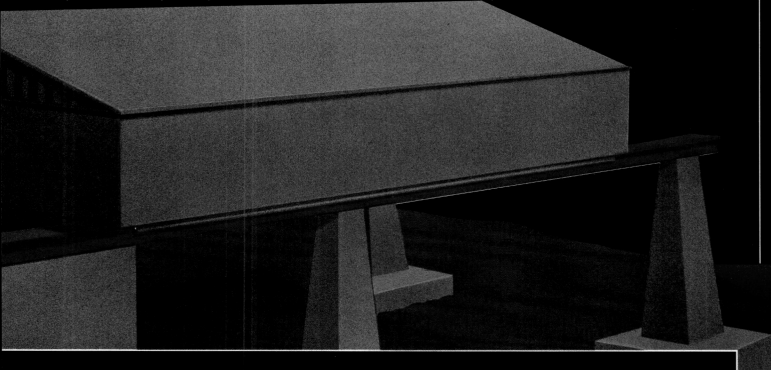

A Hierarchy of Computers

Each of the observatory's telescope computers is linked to the site computer. After opening the roof to begin the night's observations, the site computer gives an "OK to run" order, instructing the other computers to activate their telescopes. Every morning, the site computer polls the telescope computers for an account of the night's activity, including numbers of successful and unsuccessful observations, and a report of the space remaining on the storage disks. Passed automatically by modem to a computer at APT headquarters, this information is used for making sure the system is functioning and for scheduling visits to retrieve data from the observatory.

By 1983, a decade after development began, the MMT was capable of aiming at a target with a precision of about one second of arc. That is, the forty-five-ton instrument can track something as small as a pinhead seen from a distance of 1,000 feet. "If you had asked astronomers what the chances were of this telescope working," said Fred Chaffee, director of the Multiple-Mirror Telescope, "most of them would have said 'very limited.' " Chaffee puts himself among the conservatives who thought that the MMT would be a disappointment.

A NEW MEANS OF SUPPORT

A second tradition-flouting decision made by the designers of the Multiple-Mirror Telescope lay in the mount for the telescope. Every large optical telescope built before the MMT was given what is called an equatorial mount. In such a mounting scheme, the telescope is raised above the horizon on one axis and turned from side to side on a second axis that is perpendicular to the Earth's equator. This configuration simplifies the tracking of stars during an observation. A motor slowly turns the telescope from east to west to compensate for the Earth's rotation, which causes the stars to move across the sky. The telescope automatically follows the paths of the stars. But constructing such a mount anywhere on Earth but at the poles is similar to building on the side of a hill. Massive and costly support structures are needed to support the enormous weight of the telescope.

The mount chosen for the MMT is much simpler. The telescope is still supported on two axes: One allows it to be tilted up and down; the second permits the telescope to swing in azimuth—that is, left and right around the points of the compass. This axis, instead of rising at an angle from the Earth's surface as it does in an equatorial mount, rises vertically, an arrangement that makes possible a base of lighter construction and lower cost. The drawback of this so-called altitude-azimuth mount is that it forfeits the elegant simplicity with which an equatorial mount tracks the stars. Now the telescope must be moved continually and at ever-changing speeds in both the altitude and azimuth directions. Without high-speed computers to control the movements, such a system would never work.

The total price tag on the Multiple-Mirror Telescope was eight million dollars, about one-third the cost of a single-mirror, equatorially mounted telescope of comparable size. With its six mirrors, the MMT has the effective light-gathering capacity of a 176-inch telescope. It is the third largest optical telescope in the world and one of the scientific bargains of the century.

The MMT has seen its widest use in the field of spectrography, which is the analysis of light from stars after separating it into its component frequencies. In this role, the MMT has been very effective at conducting deep-space surveys of the distribution of galaxies on the very largest scale. In a deep-space survey, researchers measure the so-called red shift of light from many extremely faint galaxies. According to a generally accepted theory first proposed by Edwin Hubble, the lines in the spectrum of light from an object in space shift toward the red end of the scale in direct proportion to the distance of the light source. By means of such red-shift analysis, deep-space surveyors are able to estimate the relative positions of galaxies and begin to piece together a three-dimensional map of the universe.

Such a map will be invaluable to astronomers. Already the scientists know that galaxies are not spread evenly through space but tend to clump together in agglomerations ranging from small groups of a few galaxies to large clusters made up of thousands. Furthermore, clusters of galaxies seem to form groups called superclusters 100 million light-years across. The details of the distribution of galaxies are directly relevant to the theories of cosmologists. For example, some cosmologists hypothesize that, within a few billion years of the Big Bang, galaxies were distributed more or less uniformly throughout the universe and gradually came together to form clusters and superclusters. Opposing theories suggest that the galaxies were born in superclusters, formed from colossal clouds of gas. By delineating the actual structure of the universe on this grandest of scales, deep-space surveys should shed light on which of the theories is correct.

So far, only about two percent of the sky has been studied in enough detail to determine how galaxies are distributed, not enough to confirm one theory or the other. The portions of the map that have been completed suggest that the universe is kind of a bubbly cosmic foam—empty spaces 60 to 150 million light-years in diameter that are defined by superclusters of galaxies that surround them like the film of soap that forms a bubble.

Computers may have made feasible the multiple-mirror approach to building a telescope, but they have also made possible the casting of mirrors that dwarf the 200-inch reflector of the Hale telescope atop Mount Palomar. Used singly or in groups in the manner pioneered by the MMT, such mirrors promise to add millions of light-years to the distance that telescopes can peer into the universe.

SPIN CASTING GIANT MIRRORS

The man responsible for the resurrection of large mirrors is Roger Angel, of the University of Arizona. His idea was to melt glass in an oven that rotates like a record-player turntable. As the oven spins, a pool of molten glass in a mold centered on the floor of the furnace begins to flow toward the walls of the mold, where the glass level begins to rise. The result is a glass disk with a parabolic surface, ideal for use as a telescope reflector.

For his first experiments in 1979, Angel melted Pyrex cups and bowls in a backyard kiln, but he quickly graduated to more substantial equipment monitored and controlled by computer. By 1985, Angel had at his disposal a 120-ton steel rotating furnace with a 480-inch-diameter turntable in a lab beneath the university football stadium. Glass in the furnace is heated to 1,200 degrees Celsius by dozens of electric heating elements placed throughout the oven to maintain a uniform temperature. These heaters are similar to those in an electric toaster, but in this use they require two megawatts of electricity—enough to power 2,000 homes for a year. Since temperature differences in the glass during heating or cooling can result in tiny flaws in the surface of the mirror as it solidifies, the temperature is monitored by a computer at hundreds of points in the glass. Throughout the casting process, the computer constantly adjusts the output of the heaters. Spin casting produces mirrors that are both relatively light and extremely rigid. This is accomplished with the use of molds that give the back of a mirror a honeycomb pattern for structural strength.

The turntable in Angel's furnace can rotate as fast as twelve times a minute. The rate of spin is also computer-monitored for precise control over the shape that the molten glass acquires. A parabolic mirror focuses light at a central point whose position is determined by the depth of the curve in the parabola. The distance from the center of the mirror to that point is called the focal length of the mirror. By adjusting the spin rate of the oven, curves of various depths—and thus mirrors having a variety of focal lengths—can be produced with the technique. The faster the spin, the deeper the curve and the closer to the mirror the light will be focused.

Mirrors with short focal length are desirable because they allow the telescopes to be more compact. Support structures for such telescopes are less costly to build, and they sway less in the buffeting wind. They also can be housed in smaller observatory buildings. Before Angel's innovation, however, short focal length has been extremely difficult to achieve in a large telescope because of the amount of the shaping necessary to produce a deep curve in the mirror. Five tons of glass were ground away in fabricating the Palomar mirror. The result was a reflector of average focal length.

However, one obstacle blocked the road to a large, short-focal-length mirror—the polishing. Rigid polishing disks of the kind used on long-focal-length mirrors are inappropriate for polishing the deeply curved surface of a mirror of short focal length. To work at all, the disks would have to be very small, about one inch in diameter. According to Angel, polishing a large mirror with disks of that size would be "about as much fun as cleaning the Washington Monument with a toothbrush." To solve the problem, mirror makers have again turned to computers. Angel has proposed to replace rigid polishing disks with disks that flex on command from a computer. Every millisecond, the computer would send two dozen commands to the polishing disk, telling it how to adapt its shape to the curvature of the mirror.

As Roger Angel pursues his vision with a spinning furnace and a computerized polisher, many in the astronomical community are watching. Four groups have already placed orders for the spin-cast mirrors—among them, the Columbus Project and the developers of the National New Technology Telescope. The Columbus Project is a collaboration of the University of Arizona, Ohio State University, the University of Chicago, and Italy's Arcetri Astrophysical Observatory in Florence. The instrument this consortium plans to produce will combine the power of two 315-inch telescopes, giving it the light-gathering potential of a 445-inch reflector. The Columbus Project is scheduled to install its telescope on Arizona's Mount Graham in 1992, the 500th anniversary of Christopher Columbus's discovery of America.

The National New Technology Telescope, a project of the National Optical Astronomy Observatories, will be an even larger instrument. It will have four 315-inch telescopes working together to provide ten times the light-gathering

One Mirror from Many

The mirror in the Keck telescope atop Hawaii's Mauna Kea has a diameter of ten meters, or nearly 400 inches. Making a reflector of this size from a single piece of glass in 1980, when the mirror was commissioned, would have presented virtually insurmountable technical difficulties. The spin-casting technique for making large mirrors that are both light-weight and rigid had not yet been developed. Casting the reflector with the technology then available, had the effort succeeded, would have resulted in glass so thick that the mirror would have sagged under its own weight, distorting its reflected images of objects in space. Furthermore, the structure required to support such a massive mirror—and to move it as the telescope tracked a star across the sky—would have been prohibitively expensive.

The Keck telescope designers avoided these problems by dividing the mirror into thirty-six hexagonal sections pieced together in a honeycomb pattern. Each segment is only six feet in diameter, three inches thick, and weighs 880 pounds. An elaborate computer-operated control system enables the pieces to work together as one mirror.

The Keck telescope's sectional mirror detects both visible and infrared light with unrivaled sensitivity, allowing astronomers to probe the origins of the universe by peering billions of light-years farther into space than was possible with earlier telescopes.

One Mirror from Many

Gold-plated sensors span the gaps between mirror segments to detect minuscule shifts in position *(left)*. As two adjacent sections become misaligned, a sensor tongue on one side of the gap moves within the sensor body on the other side, altering an electrical characteristic of the sensor called capacitance *(inset)*. Twice a second, computers check the capacitance of each sensor to detect shifts in mirror position. Computers respond with commands to actuators that control the three whiffletrees that support each mirror on steel rods as thin as a pencil lead *(below)*. Coordinated by computer, the whiffletrees shift mirror segments by as little as four nanometers.

Tongue

Body

Actuator

Whiffletree

Rod

Maintaining the Perfect Hyperbola

For the Keck telescope's mirror to focus images of distant galaxies and other objects deep in space on the instrument's detectors, the thirty-six sections must form an almost perfect hyperbola. Yet as the telescope is elevated or rotated to track a target, gravity tends to pull individual segments out of position. The instrument can perform properly only if deviations in the mirror's surface are kept smaller than the wavelengths of light, which means that the alignment of the mirror sections must be maintained within a few nanometers, or billionths of a meter.

Delicate electronic sensors and precise mechanical positioning devices attached to the underside of each section allow a computer network to monitor and control the shape of the mirror. The system employs 168 sensors, which are distributed along the narrow gaps between mirror segments. Each segment is held in place by three finely adjustable supports called whiffletrees.

Mirror-Analysis Computer

Communications Computer

Scheduling Computer

Input/Output Computer

Master Computer

A baker's dozen of computers control the alignment of the Keck telescope's mirror segments. The sensors and actuators for each section of glass are linked to the system through thirty-six node boxes. The devices translate sensor readings into digital signals for the nine input/output computers, one for every four mirror segments, and relay commands to the actuators from the mirror-analysis computer, which analyzes all the sensor data and calculates the adjustments needed to keep the segments properly aligned. A communications computer manages this exchange of information between the other units, while a scheduling computer monitors the operation of the entire system. Technicians use the master computer to check whether the other computers are performing satisfactorily.

power of the 200-inch telescope at Mount Palomar. This telescope will be installed on Mauna Kea in Hawaii.

According to Fred Chaffee of the MMT, however, more is at stake than a few orders for Angel's mirrors. "Upon Roger's success or failure," said Chaffee, "depends the direction of optical astronomy for the next century." That may be, but not all astronomers are betting their chips on either the new lightweight mirrors or the multiple-telescope concept. They look to satellite-mounted telescopes in Earth orbit, where the absence of an interfering atmosphere makes a modest-size telescope in space as revealing as the largest instrument on Earth.

ATMOSPHERIC INTERFERENCE

All objects viewed through earthbound optical telescopes are blurred to some degree by the erratic motions of small cells of air, ten to twenty centimeters across, that are caused by temperature and density variations in the atmosphere. The effect of this turbulence is distortion, readily seen with the naked eye on any clear night: The stars twinkle.

In the past, astronomers have been unable to do anything but complain about this nuisance, though some have tried remedial action. The eccentric Swiss astrophysicist Fritz Zwicky is said to have once ordered a night assistant at Palomar to fire a rifle in the direction the telescope was pointing. His idea was that the bullet would punch a hole in the atmosphere and improve the seeing conditions. When that did not work, he suggested that a jet airplane be hired to fly over the observatory to clear the air. There is no record of that ploy ever being tested.

Zwicky's odd notions notwithstanding, astronomers became convinced that there is only one certain way to overcome the effects of the atmosphere: To put the telescope above the problem—in space, where the stars do not twinkle. The solution is embodied in the soon-to-be-launched Hubble Space Telescope, named for Edwin Hubble of Mount Wilson fame. The designers of the Space Telescope decided from the outset to take maximum advantage of the clear view above the atmosphere. They commissioned the Perkin-Elmer Corporation of Danbury, Connecticut, to manufacture a mirror 94.5 inches in diameter and so perfectly formed that it would focus light more than ten times as accurately as any previous mirror.

The exacting task of producing such a mirror was made doubly difficult by the worrisome fact that the polishing process would have to be accomplished on Earth, under the influence of gravity, whereas the finished product would be used in a zero-gravity environment. Technicians at Perkin-Elmer realized that the mirror, cast in the shape of a shallow bowl, would sag under its own weight as it was polished. When the warping disappeared in the weightlessness of space, they feared that the mirror would no longer conform to the exacting, few-parts-per-billion specifications of the astronomers. In an effort to compensate for the tug of the Earth, a team of fifty Perkin-Elmer engineers spent three years building an "anti-gravity" machine to simulate as closely as possible the gravity-free environment of Earth orbit. The device consisted of 138 vertical rods supporting the underside of the mirror. The rod underneath each section of the mirror was lifted by springs or counterweights with a force exactly equal to the weight of that portion of the glass. While the engineering involved was relatively simple, it was extraordinarily challenging to make this system work with the precision that was needed. A computer was used to calculate minute effects such as variations in the thickness and stiffness of the glass, friction in the rod mechanisms, and errors in setting the positions of the rods.

With the mirror in effect freed from gravity, a computer-controlled polisher went to work. As the polishing head, which is several inches in diameter, moved across the mirror, the computer guided it in leveling out the hills and valleys of the surface. Each polishing run lasted a day or two. Then the mirror surface was scanned with a laser, and data on its smoothness was fed into the computer. A contour map resulted, showing the remaining hills and valleys. Using this computer-generated map, the Perkin-Elmer technicians programmed the system for another polishing run. After twenty-five such cycles, the mirror-polishing team had produced the most nearly perfect large mirror in the world.

The Hubble telescope, because of its fine mirror and unique vantage point, is expected to significantly advance the field of astronomy on many fronts. Perhaps the most exciting prospect is for images that the orbiting instrument will collect from the deepest reaches of space and time. Project scientists hope that data from the Hubble telescope will at last enable cosmologists to explain how galaxies are formed, to gauge how old the universe is, and to reveal whether the cosmos is finite or infinite. Among other things, the telescope will peer into the central regions of galaxies in search of conclusive evidence for black holes, and scrutinize stars for captive planets like those of the Solar System.

GETTING THE TWINKLE OUT

In 1970, long before construction of the Hubble Space Telescope began, a French scientist named Antoine Labeyrie pioneered an ingenious technique that has since enabled astronomers to undertake some of the Hubble's assignments here on Earth. Labeyrie invented a way to unscramble light waves that have already passed through the atmosphere—to get rid of the twinkle. The Frenchman's procedure allows an earthbound telescope to search for planets in orbit around distant suns and probe the mysteries of suns that revolve around each other. It also permits astronomers to make some celestial measurements, such as the diameters of stars and the distances between close neighbors, that had previously been all but impossible because of atmospheric blurring.

Labeyrie was not an astronomer by training. He was a physicist with a post in the optical sciences program of the State University of New York at Stony Brook, where he had been working with lasers. Labeyrie's insight came from a phenomenon familiar to many experimenters in this field: If a plate of glass, roughened by grinding, is placed in the path of a laser beam, a multiple image of the laser beam results. When focused by a lens on a photographic plate, the result is a sheet of film speckled with images of the laser beam. The speckles are produced when light rays from different parts of the beam are refracted, or bent, in varying directions as they pass through imperfections in the glass and then are focused in different places by the lens.

Labeyrie theorized that the atmosphere may do the same thing to the starlight that reaches a telescope. This insight was highly intuitive, since Labeyrie had never looked through a large telescope. But it also had a certain roundabout logic: Because stars are so far away, they are basically points of light, and their beams have some of the same physical properties as the beam of a laser. Labeyrie knew, however, that there would be an important difference. Unlike the flaws in ground glass, the chance imperfections in the atmosphere change constantly, causing the speckles to move about in an unpredictable fashion. Since a picture of the heavens typically requires an exposure of several hours, the speckles would appear as an uninformative blur. Labeyrie calculated that an exposure time of no more than one-thirtieth of a second would be necessary to stop the speckles in their tracks—quite a radical idea to astronomers accustomed to letting light slowly build up on their photographic plates.

Dramatic pictures were not Labeyrie's goal, however; he simply needed a good clear look at the speckles. He knew that the arrangement of speckles would appear to be a meaningless jumble because of the effects of the atmosphere, but he guessed that it would hold a telltale pattern nonetheless. If his hunch proved correct, the overall size of the speckle pattern and, in some cases, the separations between individual speckles would be determined by another type of distortion different from that produced by atmospheric turbulence. Diffraction, as this distortion is called, is inherent to the optics of the telescope mirror and is well understood. The layout of the speckles would hold an easily decipherable code to the actual image of a star. Labeyrie called his concept speckle interferometry.

Labeyrie wrote to Horace Babcock, then head of Mount Palomar Observatory, asking for time on the Palomar telescope to try out these ideas, but his request was greeted with skepticism. Part of the problem was that no astronomer at Palomar had ever heard of the Frenchman. Robert Stachnik, who at the time was a graduate student in astronomy at Stony Brook, recalled that Babcock contacted the Astronomy Department about "some crazy French guy," in Stachnik's words, "who claimed he wanted to get on the Palomar telescope to produce diffraction images." Stachnik, Daniel Gezari, also a graduate student, and Stephen Strom, then a professor of astronomy at Stony Brook, visited Labeyrie. After the interview, the three astronomers agreed that Labeyrie "seemed to make some kind of sense." Vouched for by Strom and two newfound collaborators, Stachnik and Gezari, Labeyrie received permission to experiment at Palomar.

A MINIMALIST APPROACH

The equipment that the Stony Brook team took with them to California was modest—a secondhand movie camera, souped up for rapid exposures. But the experiments worked like a charm. "We could see speckles bright as day," Stachnik recalls. Not only did the researchers film the multiple images that Labeyrie had predicted, but they immediately put the captured speckles to scientific use. Using a rather complex analytic technique, which involved shining a laser through the developed film, refocusing the beam, and measuring the resulting distortion in the speckle pattern, they could calculate just how large the undistorted image should be. With this approach they were able to measure the diameters of a number of supergiant stars. Fifty years earlier, Albert Michelson, one of the founders of modern optical physics, had accomplished this feat for the same stars measured by Labeyrie and his colleagues. But Michelson's experimental instruments—called stellar interferometers, by no great coincidence—had required such extreme structural precision that they had never been practical for wider use.

Speckle interferometry had yielded important scientific results almost instantly, and astronomers took note. Thanks to Labeyrie, they had suddenly acquired the ability to make measurements of bright objects about thirty times more accurately than before. Since then, astronomers have applied the technique at several dozen observatories, and research continues at a number of sites. Most of the development work focuses on building camera systems capable of photographing faint stars, without prolonging the exposure times.

All of the research teams have one thing in common: In place of the Labeyrie method, of shining a laser through film, they use computers to analyze speckle patterns. Once the patterns are digitized, a computer can superimpose on one another, in a process called stacking, several thousand speckle patterns from successive exposures. The results are very precise representations of stars, suitable for further analysis. There is hope among researchers that stacking will provide pictures of the surfaces of stars.

The most productive use of speckle interferometry has been in studying the multitude of binary star systems that populate the Milky Way galaxy. A binary system consists of a pair of stars that orbit each other under the influence of their mutual gravitational attraction. Knowing the average distance between the stars and how long they take to complete one orbit allows astronomers to calculate the mass of the individual stars. Star mass is important to astronomers because virtually every property of a star—its brightness, the rate at which it expends its fuel, and the probability that it will eventually explode or, alternatively, burn out—depends on mass. The essence of the speckle-interferometry technique for determining mass is in measuring the separations between thousands of pairs of speckles. The distance between members of many of the pairs will not fall into any pattern, but the gap between the majority will be identical, a distance that corresponds to the space between the two stars. Thus, by measuring the gap between speckles at many points in the course of at least one complete orbit, the scientist can calculate the two factors needed to pin down the mass of the stars.

According to Harold McAlister of Georgia State University, an authority on binary star interferometry, "The computer essentially made it possible to push this technique to its limits by carrying out very complicated calculations on each and every one of tens of thousands of pictures." The superior resolution available through speckle interferometry has unmasked many points of light in the heavens for what they really are—binary star systems that twinkled like single objects without Labeyrie's technique. The success in identifying binary systems has convinced many astronomers that speckle interferometry will lead to the first discoveries of planets in orbit around stars other than the Sun.

A NEW BREED OF DETECTORS

Photographic film was sensitive enough to freeze speckle patterns for Antoine Labeyrie, the essential step that made speckle interferometry possible. But it was clear to astronomers in other branches of research—and to those who computerized Labeyrie's technique—that the photographic materials long in use at observatories were far from ideal as detectors. Much of the energy that strikes a plate is lost in chemical reactions in the photographic emulsion. In the process, the very faintest objects in the view of a telescope tend to disappear. During the 1950s and 1960s, when the development of new optical tools for astronomy was at a virtual standstill, many scientists turned their attention to producing better detectors.

A crucial step that benefited this effort actually occurred near the turn of the century. The work of Albert Einstein and others showed that the energy of light—which is delivered in packets called photons—can be transferred to electrons by a phenomenon called the photoelectric effect. The energized electrons constitute an electrical signal that can be amplified and recorded.

By the 1950s, this process had been incorporated into a device called the photomultiplier tube, which was ten to twenty times more efficient at collecting light than a photographic plate. Photomultiplier tubes were limited in that they could only look at one star at a time and could not, by themselves, record an image. Usually their output was recorded on a chart with a rising or falling line to show the brightness of each star observed. In the 1960s and 1970s, the same technology employed in television picture tubes was adapted to meet the more exacting demands of astronomers. These sensors—called vidicons—combined the efficiency of photomultiplier tubes with the image-recording abilities of photographic plates.

Meanwhile, the explosive development of microelectronic technology had produced a detector that would rapidly supplant all of its predecessors—the charge-coupled device. CCDs, as the new detectors were dubbed from the start, are elegant little chips of semiconducting silicon about the size of postage stamps. Wherever light strikes the surface, a small amount of electrical charge accumulates. By measuring the charge that builds up in each section of the chip—called a picture element, or pixel—it is possible to estimate accurately the amount of light striking there. The CCDs used by astronomers have hundreds of thousands of pixels and thus are capable of recording very detailed images. CCDs are roughly 100 times more sensitive than the finest photographic plates, allowing astronomers to see ten times farther out into the universe. And like photographic film, they can be made sensitive to X rays, or to infrared or ultraviolet light *(pages 33-35)*.

The charge-coupled device was invented in 1970 at Bell Telephone Laboratories by Willard S. Boyle and George E. Smith. Their initial idea had nothing to do with starlight or counting photons. They were building a device for computer memory circuits, which could store a small electrical impulse in various tiny compartments and read out the charges later. But the chips that Boyle and Smith came up with could only be read sequentially in rows; they did not offer random access, which was important for computer memories. It became apparent that they were much better suited to imaging applications in which random access was unnecessary. Researchers explored the idea of making CCDs the eyes of a so-called picture phone—a telephone that would link callers by sight as well as by sound. The project was abandoned, however, when consumer surveys revealed that the projected cost of the phones would be higher than the market would bear.

The Bell Labs CCD team dispersed, and the concept was picked up by other electronics companies, notably Texas Instruments. CCDs eventually found their way into a wide assortment of electronic applications, such as light meters for still cameras and image recorders for video cameras. But they made their debut early on in astronomy with a Texas Instruments CCD manufactured in 1973. The

Retinas of Silicon

The silicon chip at right is a charge-coupled device, or CCD—a type of light-sensitive integrated circuit that was first applied to astronomy in 1973 and has since become indispensable at observatories around the world. The allure of the CCD lies not in its resolution (it is no better than a photographic plate in detecting small objects in space) but in its sensitivity. CCDs are up to one hundred times more responsive to light than the photographic emulsions used for astronomical observations. As few as ten photons can stimulate sensitive CCDs to begin forming a picture, whereas a photographic plate typically must absorb several hundred photons before it reacts. An image that might require a photographic exposure of two hours can be created by a CCD in a few minutes—with time to spare for other observations. Equipped with a CCD, a telescope having a mirror as small as twenty inches in diameter can perform observations once possible only with the largest telescopes, such as the 200-inch Hale telescope on Mount Palomar in California.

The price for these benefits is high. The CCD chip itself, made in small quantities, can cost many thousands of dollars. In addition, a fast and powerful computer with a capacious memory—as well as a great deal of other electronic equipment—is necessary to convert the electrical signals in the CCD's pixels into an image (*overleaf*). At a rate of approximately two bytes per pixel, a CCD that contains 640,000 pixels produces an image that occupies more than a million bytes of computer memory or storage space. More than twelve million bytes of data might be produced during a night's observing, including calibration results and other information. Such a CCD intercepts only one percent of the image produced by a telescope. Larger CCDs—or a mosaic of small ones for capturing more of the image—would create an additional profusion of data.

The number of images that CCDs are capable of producing would overwhelm astronomers' capacity to analyze them without additional help from computers. To this end, programmers at Bell Laboratories have developed the Faint Object Classification and Analysis System (FOCAS), a library of software that automatically classifies stars and other heavenly bodies according to magnitude, type, and other factors, and that can even tell whether something that appears to be a large object is actually a cluster of smaller ones.

Two views of the heavens. The appeal of the CCD to astronomers is evident from these images, made of the same section of the sky through the 158-inch telescope at the Cerro Tololo Interamerican Observatory in Chile. At far left, a photograph shows a sky populated by a handful of bright objects—distant galaxies and stars, for the most part. The CCD, because of its superior sensitivity to light, reveals hundreds of additional galaxies, many of them farther than ten billion light-years from Earth and never before detected by any kind of telescope.

Making an exposure. Photons *(yellow balls)* striking the surface of a nine-pixel CCD at left are converted by the photoelectric effect into electrons *(red balls)*. Initially these are randomly distributed within each of the CCD's potential wells *(light blue squares)*. A well is divided into three troughs which are electrically isolated. After the exposure, voltage is applied to each potential well to move all the electrons into the uppermost trough *(below)*.

Transferring the charge. Computer-controlled voltage differences between troughs cause electrons to migrate, one trough at a time, toward the CCD's output register *(dark blue squares)*. First, high voltage is applied to the trough containing the electrons to repel them toward the center trough, which is supplied with a lower voltage. High voltage at the third trough prevents the electrons from entering. The computer then shifts the voltages to move the electrons into the third trough. With the third application of this technique, all the electrons have been moved one pixel downward, except for those in the bottom row; they are herded into the leftmost trough of the output register.

Processing a CCD Image

A CCD works on the principle of photoelectricity. That is, the chip is designed to produce and store electrical charges when it is exposed to light. The device, shown schematically on these pages, is made of a wafer-thin layer of pure silicon that has been deliberately processed to impart different electrical properties to different areas of the surface.

When light strikes a pixel, the silicon surface responds by ejecting electrons into an underlying collection area called a potential well, where they form a latent image. Like the latent image of a photograph, a CCD image must be developed. In this technology, however, the processing is done by computer, rather than in a darkroom chemical bath. And, while a photograph is developed all at once, a CCD image must be processed one pixel at a time. As shown on these pages, converting a CCD's electrical charges into a picture is ac-

complished by means of charge coupling, a technique that links each charge with a particular pixel and from which the CCD takes its name.

The electrons collected in each potential well are shifted from one pixel to the next, moving toward an output register along the side of the CCD, just outside the light-sensitive area. The output register then shifts the electrons to a measuring device consisting of an amplifier and an analog-to-digital converter. The amplifier boosts the strength of the electrical charge carried by each batch of electrons, and the converter measures the amplified charge. When the process is complete, the computer has stored in memory the brightness recorded at each pixel—information it can use to generate points of light to be displayed on a television screen or recorded on photographic paper.

Recording the pixels. When the output register is full, migration of electrons across the CCD ceases while the batches of electrons are moved, trough by trough, toward the amplifier *(arrow)*. There, the electrical charge carried by each electron batch is boosted and passed to the analog-to-digital converter. This device assigns each voltage a numerical value as high as 650,000. The numbers, which represent the intensity of the light striking the bottom row of pixels, are stored in the computer's memory, and the electrons in the next row of pixels are transferred to the output register. This process continues until light intensities for all the pixels have been stored in the computer.

device was produced for space scientists at the Jet Propulsion Laboratory (JPL) in Pasadena, California, so that it could be considered for a possible role in space-probe missions.

ASTRONOMICAL CONSERVATIVES

One JPL scientist, James Janesick, was certain that CCDs were the wave of the future. But he worried that the astronomical community would take a cautious, wait-and-see approach. "Astronomers are a pretty hard group to convince," he says. "It's very, very hard to make them change." In his view, it was essential that the new technology be included in the planning stages of important new projects like the space telescope, which was no more than a NASA proposal at the time. To build enthusiasm for CCDs, Janesick collaborated with James Westphal of the California Institute of Technology in constructing a CCD camera system and demonstrating it for astronomers at major observatories. Westphal's participation was important, because he was involved at the time with a panel of notable astronomers commissioned to develop an imaging system for the space telescope.

Between them, the two scientists carried the day, much helped by some stunning early achievements by the CCD: In 1975, scientists from the Jet Propulsion Laboratory and the University of Arizona in Tucson used the sixty-one-inch telescope on nearby Mount Lemmon to make a CCD image of the planet Uranus. The CCD improved the resolution of the sixty-one-inch telescope to such a degree that its performance was equivalent to a 400-inch reflector focusing an image on a photographic plate. Another successful test, this time at the 200-inch telescope on Mount Palomar, convinced the majority of astronomers, and NASA decided to use a CCD imaging system in the Hubble Space Telescope. Today, CCD cameras are employed at every major observatory. A typical CCD for scientific use has over 150,000 pixels. The custom-built chips for the Hubble telescope have more than 640,000 pixels, and the numer of pixels in the next generation of CCDs will exceed four million.

As helpful to astronomers as the CCD's remarkable powers of resolution is the device's ability to register a wide range of brightnesses. For example, an image of a galaxy recorded on a photographic plate can only accommodate about a hundredfold difference in brightness between its faintest and most brilliant parts. In practice, radiant central regions of galaxies are often overexposed—and thus show no detail—in order to record the dim outer portions. Or the far reaches of a galaxy are sacrificed for the sake of detail at the center. CCDs, however, can record dim objects that are 10,000 times fainter than the brightest star in a telescope's field of view. One application of this capability has been to study the relationships between all the visible elements in galaxies. Such analysis helped confirm evidence that many—and perhaps all—galaxies are much more massive than was previously believed. The speed at which stars move in the dim outer regions is simply too great for them to be held in orbit by the gravity of the mass visible at galactic centers. The only possible explanation is the presence of a great deal of matter that does not give off visible light.

Cosmologists—scientists who study the universe as a whole—are particularly grateful for the CCD. For example, Hyron Spinrad and his colleagues at the University of California at Berkeley have used a CCD camera with the 120-inch telescope on Mount Hamilton in northern California to find exceedingly faint and distant galaxies. In early 1987, Spinrad observed an object, known only by its radio identification 3C326.1, that is at least 10 billion light-years away. It contains large amounts of gas and very few stars, leading Spinrad to conjecture that he has detected light beamed from a galaxy that is still in the process of forming. Other possible protogalaxies—ones that some astronomers believe may be as far away as 17 billion light-years—were detected by University of Arizona astronomer Richard Elston in the spring of 1987, during field tests of a new infrared CCD device.

PUTTING THE DATA TO USE

While CCDs were unquestionably a major leap forward, they exacerbated an already-critical problem: Astronomers were finding themselves painfully ill equipped to analyze the data they were becoming so efficient at gathering. The CCDs in use at most observatories generate a trove of information, equivalent to the contents of an encyclopedia, in the course of a single night's viewing. To be of any value, this data must be processed, stored, and made available to scientists in some commonly understandable format. Making the data accessible would be an impossible task without powerful, high-speed computers. Even with the aid of such machines, analyzing the flood of information tends to run far behind the assembling of it.

An example of the kinds of data-processing problems that astronomers encounter is that the "raw" images from a CCD are not realistic. An area may actually be brighter or dimmer than it appears because individual pixels of a CCD have varying sensitivities to light. To deal with this lack of consistency, observers use a technique called flat fielding. They make an exposure of a uniform source of light, such as the sky at dawn. They can then map variations among the CCD's pixels and, with the help of a computer, scale the brightness data recorded at each pixel either up or down depending on the findings in the flat-field exposure.

This procedure is just one of many facets of another major function of computers in astronomy: image processing. The output from an electronic detector—such as a CCD—is not an image like a photograph. It is a two-dimensional array of numbers, like a huge bingo card. Every modern observatory must have at its disposal a sophisticated system of software that enables astronomers to transform this array of numbers into an image and then modify the picture in various ways. For example, astronomers routinely make use of such techniques as heightening contrast, zooming in on important details, and adding color to black-and-white images. In the words of Don Wells, one of the pioneers in this field, the task of the image-processing software is to "bring the bits back to life."

Astronomical image processing had its roots in the space program in the mid-1960s. By necessity, the images taken by NASA's planetary probes had to be digitized and radioed to Earth. An image-processing laboratory was set up at the Jet Propulsion Laboratory in 1969 with precision cathode-ray tubes to display the pictures reconstructed from the data received from space. A precision CRT is essentially a high-resolution television picture tube with a built-in lens to focus images on photographic film. In order to study faint but significant features in these images, such as craters on Mercury or bands in the atmosphere of Jupiter, techniques were developed for enhancing the colors and contrast. One common practice is the use of false-color images. A black-and-white image taken of Jupiter's satellite Io, for example, is transmitted to Earth as a grid of numbers expressing the brightness of Io at various points on its surface. The number 100 might correspond to the brightest spot and zero to the blackness of space around the satellite. A false color image is created by assigning different colors to different numbers in this range—blue to numbers between 90 and 100, green to numbers between 80 and 90, and so on. A false color image enables the scientist to pick out details that are difficult to see in the subtle shadings of gray in a black-and-white image.

ONE CHUNK AT A TIME

The image processing done at the Jet Propulsion Laboratory in the 1960s and early 1970s was batch oriented. That is, the data to be processed would go to a computing center in the form of decks of punched cards or reels of magnetic tape. The computing center would generate instructions for the image-processing and photographic laboratories, which would return the pictures the following day. The space scientists would then examine the results; if they decided that the images needed additional enhancement, they would try once again and the next day see slightly improved pictures.

Batch processing was the norm when Don Wells arrived at Kitt Peak National Observatory in 1973. Wells, however, was familiar with digital imaging techniques. His thesis adviser at the University of Texas, an astronomer named Gerard de Vaucouleurs, had seen the potential in the earliest image-processing experiments at JPL and realized that computers would be important in this role. Two developments were forcing astronomers to deal more and more with digital arrays of numbers rather than with simple photographs. For the most part, photographic plates were being phased out in favor of the various pre-CCD electronic detectors—vidicons and photomultiplier tubes—that produced digital readouts. And photographs still being taken were often turned into digital data with scanners, which read the density of exposed grains in the emulsion at all points on a plate. In either case, the astronomer was left with a digital array, and no convenient way to manipulate the numbers or enhance the image.

De Vaucouleurs had begun practicing digital image-processing techniques in the mid-1960s, and Wells, as a graduate student, had learned along with his mentor. "As a result," he recalls, "I knew what was wrong with all the current technology." And he knew what kinds of improvements to make. "I wanted to do real-time interaction with the programs and the data. I did not want to submit card decks. I wanted to type new commands on the keyboard."

In 1974, Wells began to build such a system at Kitt Peak with a team of

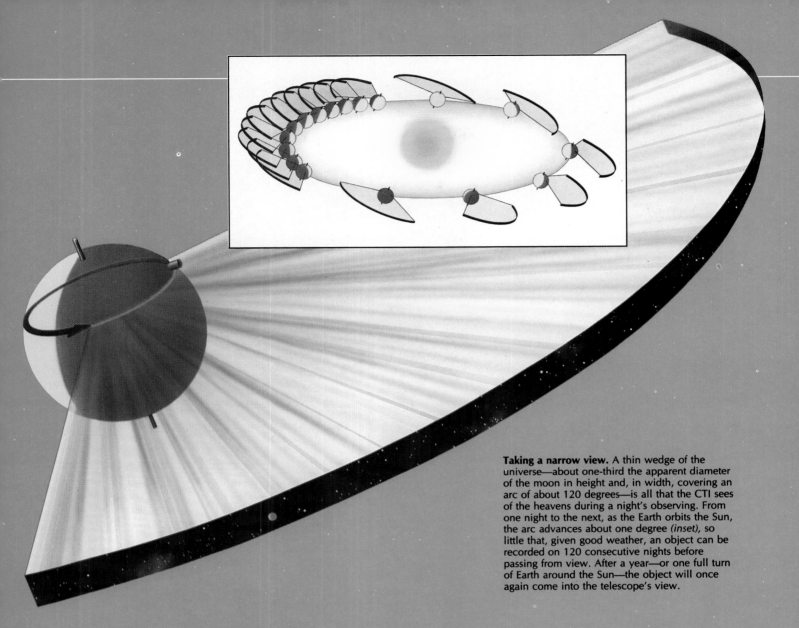

Taking a narrow view. A thin wedge of the universe—about one-third the apparent diameter of the moon in height and, in width, covering an arc of about 120 degrees—is all that the CTI sees of the heavens during a night's observing. From one night to the next, as the Earth orbits the Sun, the arc advances about one degree *(inset)*, so little that, given good weather, an object can be recorded on 120 consecutive nights before passing from view. After a year—or one full turn of Earth around the Sun—the object will once again come into the telescope's view.

A Strip of Stars and Galaxies

On Kitt Peak near Tucson, Arizona, stands an unusual telescope called the Charge-Coupled Device/Transit Instrument, or CTI. Instead of tracking stars across the sky as most telescopes do, the CTI sits unmoving as the heavens slip past. The CTI is looking for supernovas, the cataclysmic explosions that end the lives of many stars. Within a few days' time, these dying suns increase ten billion times in brightness and blast great volumes of debris into interstellar space.

Understanding supernovas is crucial to explaining many aspects of stellar evolution, from the availability of heavier elements to the effects of cosmic shock waves. To acquire such insight, astronomers would prefer to observe supernovas from their earliest moments, a rare opportunity because no one can predict whether a particular star is about to undergo a paroxysmic death.

Charge-coupled devices, or CCDs *(pages 33-35)*, and computers have provided a solution: to focus a telescope on the same part of the sky night after night in the hope that a supernova will occur there. The success of the idea depends on the extraordinary light sensitivity of the CCD. Used in place of photographic film as a detector for a telescope, the CCD records much fainter objects and does so with an exposure time of only a minute or so, compared to an hour for film. The blurring that results even from an exposure as short as sixty seconds is compensated for electronically.

Although the telescope monitors only a narrow swath of sky *(above)*, the CCD collects about 450 million bytes of data each night, all of which must be examined for supernovas—as well as for other objects of interest, such as quasars and variable stars—before the next night's observations. To accomplish this requires an immense amount of computing power *(overleaf)*.

The mountain file. Samples of data in the mountain file are displayed on a monitor to be examined visually for evidence of telescope or CCD malfunction. Variations in background luminosity during the night are measured and subtracted. Light intensities for CCD pixels struck by cosmic rays are reset to a value obtained by averaging the values of nearby pixels. The data is then archived on an optical disk capable of storing two weeks' observations.

The observations file. Data in the mountain file is analyzed. Brightness levels attributable to objects in space (and not caused by coincidental accumulations of background luminosity) are extracted, assigned coordinates according to their positions, and stored in an observations file. Data from this file is then merged with information from all the preceding nights' observations stored in the master file and the history file. Then the observations file is erased in preparation for the next night's operations.

The master file. This list of all the objects ever detected by the CTI is updated daily from the observations file. The main function of the master file is to maintain a record of each object's average luminosity, based on all the readings ever taken by the CTI. This average value is the figure the computers use for comparison when looking for changes in brightness that might signal a supernova. This list is cross-referenced to the history file.

The history file. This data base, instead of averaging observations for each object, maintains the result of each sighting separately. Should a computer comparison of average luminosity and one night's brightness suggest that a supernova may be under way, an astronomer can confirm the event by considering the unusually high value in relation to the object's brightness history.

Making Sense of the Data

Instructions for finding a supernova are easy: Photograph the same piece of the sky on consecutive nights and compare each photograph with the one taken the preceding night. If a dim object suddenly becomes blindingly bright or an object appears where none has been seen before, a supernova is the likely explanation. CTI astronomers hope to find up to 100 supernovas per year this way.

The difficulty of the task lies in the number of comparisons that must be made between observations. Each night, the CTI records the brightness of as many as 500,000 objects. Upon examination, some of those specks of light prove not to be objects at all: for example, a cosmic ray that strikes a CCD pixel registers as an extremely bright dot. And abrupt brightness increases can be tricky: A pair of objects, easily distinguishable on a night of good "seeing," as astronomers say, may merge on another night into a single, misleading object. Because of these and other anomalies, each batch of data from the CTI must be exhaustively scrutinized

and evaluated before it can be of any use to astronomers.

Doing so is the job of the CTI Daily Analysis Logging system (DAL), a battery of computer programs running on a Data General computer in Tucson. DAL's raw material is a magnetic tape of data from the telescope's CCD. Information from the beginning of each tape is displayed on a computer monitor to be certain that the telescope was operating satisfactorily; then the data is transferred to disk for processing. At this point, the night's observations are known as the mountain file. As described above, this file undergoes a thorough culling before it is used to update DAL's master file and history file, which constitute the system's data base of astronomical facts.

Astronomers can extract information from the data base by means of a comprehensive query language. The example at right is typical of a search for supernovas. DAL accepts queries directly from a keyboard, or it may be programmed to answer a query on a regular schedule, freeing astronomers from the nuisance of having to type the query repeatedly.

Find stars that have varied from their average brightnesses by more than ten times the amount that could result from measurement errors alone.

Quizzing the data base. An instruction intended to find supernova candidates—and translated into plain English from DAL's query language—appears on a computer monitor (*above*). Upon accepting the request, the computer searches the history file for such objects. In this instance, the records of five stars are extracted from the history file, each one containing information similar to the data shown for the first: the date of the observation, numbered from the first day of CTI operation; the luminosity of the object; and the possible error in each night's brightness measurements. The computer selected this star because, on day 1,050, it brightened enough to satisfy the astronomer's conditions, although subsequent dimming suggests that the star will not become a supernova. To facilitate comparison, graphs of all five stars' luminosities appear on the computer monitor below.

Day Number	Luminosity	Luminosity Error
1002	1328	± 121
1020	1189	± 127
1050	2337	± 31
1055	1173	± 114

astronomers, engineers, and computer specialists. Within four years they had produced a hardware-software combination known as the Interactive Picture Processing System (IPPS), which became a prototype for image processing facilities in observatories around the world. At the heart of the special-purpose system, Wells linked a Varian V74 minicomputer to the CDC 6400, which was the main computer at Kitt Peak. The Varian controlled a panel of peripherals, all of which were commercially available for other scientific uses, so that Wells did not have to custom-build any of his components. An IPPS workstation included a magnetic disk for storing processed pictures, a high-quality image display, and an interactive graphics terminal at which the operator issued commands to the system software. For producing hard-copy images, IPPS had a printer and a precision cathode-ray tube. The software for IPPS allowed the Kitt Peak astronomers to perform complex image-processing operations in a matter of minutes.

Computerized, interactive image processing has come to play a crucial role in every field of astronomy, and image-processing systems have evolved in step with the dramatic changes in computer technology. At the National Optical Astronomy Observatory, IPPS has been succeeded by a system called IRAF, for Image Reduction and Analysis Facility. IRAF is also now in use at many other observatories, including the Space Telescope Science Institute, the command center for the Hubble telescope. Originally designed to run on Digital Equipment's VAX computers, IRAF can now be used on many other systems as well, including Cray supercomputers.

The emergence of powerful personal computers has set the stage for the next significant development in image processing—networking. Ron Allen, who helped develop a system called GIPSY (Groningen Image Processing System) for the Westerbork Radio Telescope in Holland, used a Digital Equipment PDP9 computer at the time. "That was the top you could buy commercially," he says. "It cost a fortune. These days, any PC on your desk could outperform one of those machines." Because of the affordability and power of today's small computers, Don Wells thinks that a new world of image processing is just around the corner: "I think we'll see a situation in which every astronomer will have his own personal image-processing system. The world of the future is workstations, all tied together in global networks, with the data and the large computers in central computer centers. The people don't go there; wires do."

In the century since Edward Pickering realized that rapid computation had a vital role to play in astronomy, the goals of astronomers have not substantially changed. They still seek to observe the universe in order to understand its workings and Earth's place in the overall scheme of things. Computers have enabled astronomers to pursue these goals at a level never dreamed of half a century ago. Scientists can look much farther into the heavens and make better records of what they see. But with new knowledge has come new questions and a realization that with optical telescopes, we are seeing only one aspect of the cosmos. Many significant and fascinating features of the universe are revealed by telescopes sensitive to wavelengths outside the optical window.

A Bundle
of Telescopes

Forty miles south of Tucson, Arizona, atop 8,550-foot Mount Hopkins, a squat, rectangular building shelters a telescope of radical design. A joint project of the University of Arizona and the Smithsonian Institution, the apparatus is called the Multiple-Mirror Telescope, or MMT, and is actually a sextet of telescopes operated as one.

From inside the observatory, the mirrors of the six instruments, held in a circular array by a framework of steel struts, gaze at the clear desert sky like an unblinking compound eye. The mirrors, each seventy-two inches in diameter, gather light from distant objects. Then the beams are brought to a common focus. The result is light-gathering power that matches the ability of a 176-inch telescope.

The MMT would be impossible without computers. One keeps the telescopes aimed at a common celestial target. Another operates a tradition-breaking mount, the system of axles and pivots that permits a telescope to track a celestial object as it moves. A third computer collects and stores data during observations. Because of the computers, the MMT is not only innovative, but it has proved itself economical as well. Six small mirrors are lighter than a single large one and less costly to manufacture, though the MMT mirrors are hand-me-downs from the U.S. Air Force. At $13 million, the telescope mount cost about one-third as much to build as a mount of the design typical for a telescope of the MMT's size.

The MMT has made significant contributions since it began operation in 1979. Astronomers are using the telescope to catalog new quasars, some of the brightest, most distant objects in the universe. And the MMT has confirmed the existence of "gravitational lenses," a phenomenon predicted by Einstein's theory of relativity in which light from a distant object is bent on the way to Earth as the rays pass through the gravitational field of a large mass.

An Observatory on a Turntable

The MMT facility is an ugly duckling among observatories. Absent is the elegant, domed structure that is traditionally associated with most of the outposts of astronomy. Instead, the telescope occupies a building that could easily be mistaken for a small factory or a warehouse were it not for the fact that the building rotates.

Even more remarkable is the telescope inside. The instrument incorporates six identical Cassegrainian-type telescopes, named for the Frenchman who invented the arrangement of mirrors inside them (below). One of the advantages of the design is compactness. The MMT is only twenty-three feet long; a telescope of similar light-gathering power built with a single mirror would be more than fifty feet long.

Under the guidance of three computers, the telescope and its protective structure become one giant instrument for probing the heavens. In operation, the observatory depends on the telescope operator to keep the MMT's combined image from degenerating into six individual ones (pages 48-49). The control room includes a bank of monitors that display, for instance, the status of the mirrors, the telescope mount, and the detectors that capture the data pouring into the observatory from the stars. Another screen allows the astronomer to take a quick look at incoming observation results before they are recorded on magnetic tape.

One Telescope from Six

Light entering any one of the six telescopes that make up the MMT first encounters a concave reflector, called the primary mirror, at the base of the structure. Focused by the primary mirror onto an adjustable secondary mirror, the light is next relayed to a third (tertiary) mirror that reflects the beam to a six-sided pyramid of mirrors called the beam combiner. There the light meets beams from the other five telescopes to form a single image that plays on a detector positioned out of sight behind the primary mirrors.

Beam Combiner

Secondary Mirror

Tertiary Mirror

Primary Mirror

Keeping pace with the telescope. Mounted on four large steel wheels that roll on a steel track, the MMT's 800-ton building rotates in unison with the telescope. As the instrument turns on its mount to track a star, a sensor between the telescope and the building commands motors to inch the structure along at the same rate as the telescope. The structure has space inside for computers, a control room, laboratories, workshops, and even a lunchroom.

A Better Mount to Track the Stars

To someone standing on the rotating Earth, the stars overhead appear to drift slowly westward. In order to keep a star in view, a telescope must have a tracking system that can compensate for this motion. The tracking method depends on the manner in which the telescope is mounted.

Almost all large telescopes are supported by a so-called equatorial mount. After being aimed at a star, the telescope needs only to be rotated about a fixed axis at a constant rate. This is readily achieved by a simple clockwork mechanism *(below)*. Such a mount is expensive, however. Constructing one is similar to extending a house beyond the rim of a ravine, a gravity-defying feat that requires substantial underpinnings to keep the structure from sliding to the bottom of the gorge.

To reduce the cost of the MMT, designers chose a different sort of support—an altitude-azimuth mount. Though easier than an equatorial mount to build, this type of mount complicates the business of tracking. As explained at right, the motions of an altitude-azimuth mount are such that a simple clockwork system cannot follow a star. Not only does the telescope need to move about both axes to track its target, but the rate at which it must turn varies with time and the telescope's position.

Without computers, there would be no such mount for the MMT. No other device could make twenty calculations per second and issue to the mount the rapid-fire instructions that are necessary to keep the telescope on target. So successful is the system that it has resulted in tracking as accurate as the best equatorial mounts.

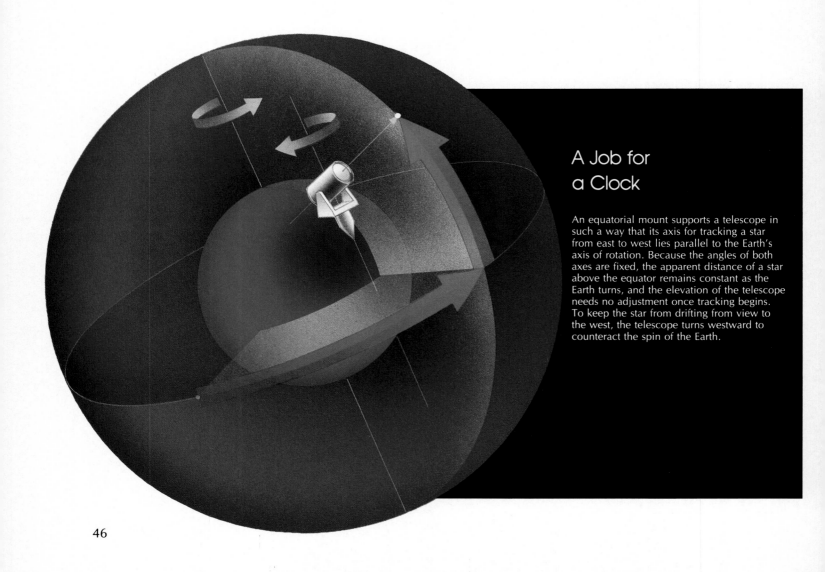

A Job for a Clock

An equatorial mount supports a telescope in such a way that its axis for tracking a star from east to west lies parallel to the Earth's axis of rotation. Because the angles of both axes are fixed, the apparent distance of a star above the equator remains constant as the Earth turns, and the elevation of the telescope needs no adjustment once tracking begins. To keep the star from drifting from view to the west, the telescope turns westward to counteract the spin of the Earth.

A job for a computer. The axis of the MMT's altitude-azimuth mount does not lie parallel to the Earth's axis of rotation, as in an equatorial mount, but instead is perpendicular to the Earth's surface. Consequently, in attempting to follow a star across the sky, the telescope drifts downward, losing the target. To compensate, the telescope must be continually elevated as it turns.

Aligning the Beams

As the elevation of the MMT changes while tracking a star, the steel structure that supports the six telescopes is deformed, primarily by the pull of gravity. Though the changes are subtle, they would quickly throw the individual images out of coincidence were it not for the Telescope Coalignment System (TCS) *(below)*. At the heart of the coalignment system is a computer dedicated to the task of continuously adjusting the tilt of the MMT's six secondary mirrors so that the images fall on top of one another—a challenging problem, ingeniously solved through a process called stacking *(right)*.

As observation of a star begins, the telescope operator roughly aligns the six images, then instructs the coalignment computer to execute a ten-second stacking program that further adjusts the secondary mirrors so that the images coincide

perfectly. To maintain this state of affairs, the TCS is programmed with an algorithm that predicts the degree of misalignment between secondary and primary mirrors from gravity and adjusts the secondary mirrors accordingly.

Because the deformation of the telescope is exceedingly complex, the algorithm lacks the precision necessary to prevent the beams from diverging, and over a period of about fifteen minutes, the combined image becomes fuzzy. The telescope operator, noting this development on a computer monitor, manually positions the secondary mirrors to readjust the six images. Manual adjustment is sufficiently accurate for spectrographic observations *(pages 50-51)*. Should an astronomer seek greater precision, however, the operator can invoke the stacking program.

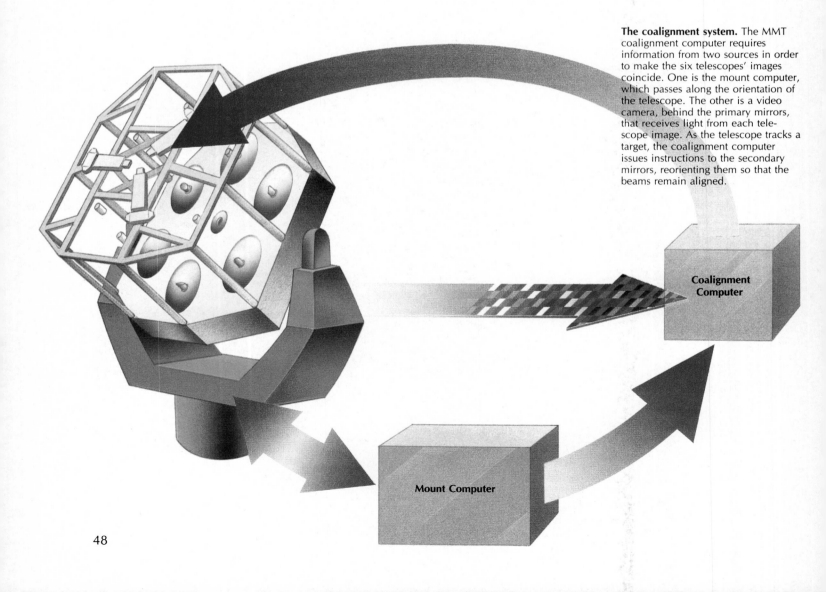

The coalignment system. The MMT coalignment computer requires information from two sources in order to make the six telescopes' images coincide. One is the mount computer, which passes along the orientation of the telescope. The other is a video camera, behind the primary mirrors, that receives light from each telescope image. As the telescope tracks a target, the coalignment computer issues instructions to the secondary mirrors, reorienting them so that the beams remain aligned.

Coalignment Computer

Mount Computer

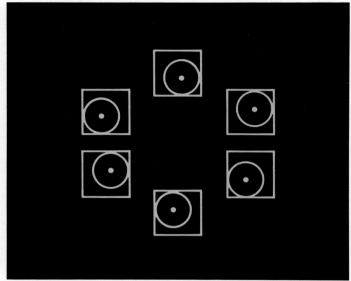

Getting to the starting point. Stacking the telescope images begins with moving the six beams of light, each represented by a circle in these illustrations, inside a square drawn on a monitor by the coalignment computer. The telescope operator accomplishes this so-called rough stack manually, by tilting the secondary mirrors from within the control room. At this point the coalignment computer takes over the stacking operation.

Identifying the beams. To identify which secondary mirror is associated with which beam, the computer draws six squares on the screen, each assigned in advance to a particular beam-and-mirror pair. Then it tilts each mirror according to a plan assured to make each beam fall within its designated square. Having identified the beams in this manner, the computer finds the brightest point in each one, called the beam's centroid *(dots)*, and stores their locations in memory. Each point and its position in the box become the basis for calibrating movement of a beam on the screen with the tilt of its mirror.

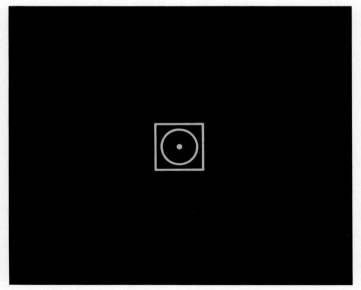

Calibrating the system. Tilting each mirror in the opposite direction and twice as far as in the preceding step, the coalignment computer relocates the centroid and notes how many pixels up or down and left or right it has moved in response to the change in mirror position. With this information, the computer can calculate how far and in which direction an increment of mirror movement shifts a beam's centroid on the computer screen. This step is designed so that the beams switch boxes *(arrows)*, eliminating the possibility of beam overlap that would confuse the calculations.

Combining the beams. Armed with the calibration between mirror tilt and centroid movement, the computer commands each secondary mirror to shift just enough to position the corresponding centroid at a preselected point on the screen, completing the stacking operation. After several minutes have passed—and before the beams have diverged so much that a rough stack is required—the telescope operator readjusts the secondary mirrors.

Detector

Concave Mirror

Convex Mirror

Aperture

Diffraction Gratings

Mirror

Collimator Lens

Inside a spectrograph. Light from the telescope enters the spectrograph through an aperture, to exclude light not coming from the target. A mirror reflects the narrow beam to a collimator lens, which makes the light rays parallel to one another and sends them toward one of three diffraction gratings, each tailored to capture a different range of wavelengths of visible light. Now in the form of a spectrum, the light is focused onto the detector by a lens assembled from a large, concave mirror and a small, convex mirror. Then the spectral data is passed to the MMT instrument computer *(arrow)*.

What the Stars Are Made Of

Most of the MMT's observing time is devoted to spectroscopy—the examination of the spectral signatures of celestial objects. Light from these sources may appear to be homogeneous, but in reality it is brighter at some wavelengths than at others. The differing intensities divulge much about the composition of luminous objects because each chemical component of a star or a galaxy reveals its presence as a series of bright or dark regions in the spectrum. Spectrographic analysis can also disclose velocity, temperature, and other characteristics.

The instrument for such research is called a spectrograph *(left)*. Aligned with the MMT's beam combiner, the detector employs a diffraction grating—a piece of glass etched with thousands of closely spaced lines—to separate light into its component wavelengths. Information is recorded on an electronic detector that works like a CCD with a single row of pixels. Unprocessed data from the spectrograph passes to the MMT's instrument computer, which also handles the operation of other observatory instruments, and thence to the astronomer in a variety of useful forms *(below)*.

Instrument Computer

MC 1331+170

Displaying the data. A spectral image arriving at the instrument computer is first stored, then displayed on a monitor as vertical lines. Their height indicates intensity; their position from left to right indicates wavelength. The display allows a quick check to assure that the telescope is observing the right target and that the detector is operating correctly. Then the data is sent to a plotter to produce a graph like that at left. A printer is available to record telescope status and observations completed.

Charting a quasar. This plot of the quasar MC 1331+170 displays spectral features typical of the high-energy objects. The tall spike at about 3,700 angstrom units signals the presence of hydrogen; the shorter one seeming to jut from its eastern slope represents nitrogen. Evenly spaced to the right are peaks for silicon and carbon. The canyon at far left in the graph is called a lyman-alpha absorption line and indicates that there is an object between the quasar and Earth, probably a galaxy rich in hydrogen, that absorbs light at a wavelength of 3,375 angstroms.

Beyond the Realm of Light

In 1927, the American Telephone and Telegraph Company transmitted the first telephone calls across the ocean by radio, a service that cost seventy-five dollars for a three-minute conversation between New York and London. At that price, connections had to be excellent. Unfortunately, they were not. Typically, callers had to shout through a steady hiss of static. Bell Laboratories was given the job of finding out why.

Among the twenty or so researchers assigned to the task was a young man named Karl Jansky, fresh out of the University of Wisconsin with a degree in physics. Jansky was dispatched to a Bell Labs facility at Holmdel, New Jersey, with instructions to isolate the source of the hiss. In the middle of a potato field, he constructed an ungainly-looking, 100-foot-long antenna made of brass pipes attached to a lumber frame. Wheels from a Model T Ford, running on a circular concrete track, supported the ends of the antenna, which was pivoted at the center so that it could be easily rotated to face in any direction. Wires from this apparatus ran to a shelter that Jansky called his shack. Inside the structure was equipment that recorded the signals detected by the antenna, freeing Jansky to work on other experiments.

After nearly a year collecting data with his radio set, Jansky discerned that the hiss was not steady at all, but that its intensity waxed and waned in an orderly manner. It was clear that the static was not caused by anything as erratic as thunderstorm activity. In fact, its source seemed to be stunningly far away. After consultations with astronomers, Jansky announced in a scientific paper that the hiss seemed to come from somewhere near the center of the Milky Way. He called it "star noise."

Jansky's find would have profound implications for the science of astronomy. In the decades that followed, scientists would move beyond the familiar informational medium of light and survey the skies across the entire spectrum of electromagnetic radiations. Not only radio waves but the electromagnetic energy of infrared and ultraviolet light, as well as X rays and gamma rays, would usher in a golden age of astronomy—one in which computers would play a grand and crucial role. Indeed, a new breed of astronomer arrived on the scene, a person often better trained in electronics and in the ways of computers than in the ancient arts of sky watching.

THE FIRST STEPS

Jansky's star noise won front-page coverage in the *New York Times* in 1933, but astronomers were slow to recognize the potential of his discovery. Comfortable with their mirrors and lenses, they had no great desire to work with radio equipment. Besides, theorists predicted at the time that radio emissions from space would be feeble. Only one amateur astronomer, a radio engineer in Illinois named Grote Reber, followed Jansky's lead. Reber built an antenna shaped like a parabolic dish (not unlike a modern television dish used to pick up satellite transmissions). His antenna was superior to Jansky's because, much as a reflector in an optical telescope focuses light, it concentrated radio waves at a single point.

Reber's antenna was about thirty feet in diameter. By aiming it in different directions and at various angles above the horizon over a period of six years, he produced the first radio maps of the Milky Way, showing radio emissions throughout the sky. But because of the modest size of the instrument, these first maps were crude, revealing only fuzzy regions of radio noise rather than well-defined sources.

The laws of physics dictate that any reflector of electromagnetic energy—whether a dish or a mirror—must have a diameter much larger than the wavelength of the incoming radiation if fine detail is to be discerned by the instrument. The diameter of the 200-inch optical reflector of the telescope at Mount Palomar, for example, is about ten million times greater than the wavelengths of visible light, resulting in superb resolution. One important radio signal, emitted by hydrogen atoms in space, has a radio wavelength of twenty-one centimeters, or about eight inches. To resolve details comparable to those seen by the 200-inch telescope, a radio dish for twenty-one-centimeter waves would have to be sixty-six miles across.

Despite this difficulty, the years just after World War II brought a leap in enthusiasm for radio astronomy. Dozens of young physicists and engineers, who had beeen trained in radio and radar technologies during the conflict, went on to apply their skills to the field pioneered by Jansky and Reber. Radio astronomy had special appeal for European astronomers, who chafed at the thick overcasts that often made optical observation of the heavens impossible. Their radio reconnaissance began to reveal facts that were unknown to optical astronomers. By the late 1940s, for example, close analysis of hydrogen transmissions from the outer reaches of the Milky Way indicated that the galaxy, like many others, had the shape of a spiral.

As the years passed, radio telescopes were built ever larger, increasing their sensitivity. In 1957, at Jodrell Bank in England, Sir Bernard Lovell constructed a radio dish that was 250 feet wide. Such huge antennas could pick up exceedingly faint whispers of radio noise, but the resolution was still so poor that the radio signals often could not be matched to an object that was visible in the sky. Nor could movable dishes be made appreciably larger than the Jodrell Bank dish; a structure much wider than 300 feet in diameter tends to sag because of its own weight.

Further size increases were possible, however, with stationary dishes, which can be supported more rigidly than a movable antenna. In 1963, Cornell University astronomers built a stationary dish 1,000 feet in diameter by lowering a radio-reflecting surface of wire netting into a limestone hollow near Arecibo, Puerto Rico. This immense parabolic dish is dependent on the Earth's movement to put various parts of the universe in view, but its resolution is about one-fourth as good as that of the unaided human eye.

WAVES IN COLLISION

Early on, radio astronomers realized that ambitious feats of engineering were not the only route to resolution. They could use electronic trickery to create the effect of a parabolic dish much larger than anything they could hope to build.

That a parabolic antenna can concentrate radio signals at all is a result of the radiation's wavelike characteristics. A radio wave from a star rebounds from an antenna in much the same way that a wave caused by dropping a stone into the water at the edge of a pond reflects from the bank. The result is a vast number of collisions between rebounding wave fronts. At some spots in front of the reflector, waves tend to cancel each other out—a phenomenon called destructive interference. At other spots, particularly at a point called the focus, waves strengthen each other—this is called constructive interference. The reflection of the incoming waves from each point on the surface of the dish contributes a small amount to the intensity and detail of the radio information received at the focus (pages 76-79).

In a process known as interferometry, resolution (but not sensitivity) can be increased by using two antennas that are situated some distance apart and linked to a central collection point. Aimed at the same source of radio signals in the sky, the two dishes can be considered as points on the rim of a single large, imaginary dish. Adding pairs of antennas between the first two supplies information from other points on the imaginary dish, further improving resolution. The parabolic curve of the imaginary radio telescope is simulated elec-

Karl Jansky tinkers with his ungainly radio antenna in a New Jersey potato field. Working for Bell Laboratories to identify the source of a persistent hiss that interfered with transatlantic telephone calls, transmitted at that time by radio, Jansky detected the first radio signals from the stars.

55

A pioneer in radio astronomy, Grote Reber stands near a reconstruction of his telescope, some thirty feet in diameter, at the National Radio Astronomy Observatory in Green Bank, West Virginia. The original instrument, built in Reber's Wheaton, Illinois, backyard in 1936, was made of wood and had a galvanized-iron surface that served as the reflector. Reber used the device to map radio sources in the Milky Way.

tronically, as if the signals from telescope pairs were being reflected toward a central focal place.

Instruments of this type achieved some remarkable success almost as soon as they went into action. In the 1950s, astronomers using a radio interferometer—the name for an assembly of cooperating radio telescopes—pinpointed the location of one of the brightest sources in the radio sky, a region they called Cygnus A. When optical astronomers looked for an object at the same spot, they found a dim speck of light. Analysis of its visible spectrum later showed the source to be a billion light-years away—an astonishing distance, considering the great strength of the radio signal. This find was the first indication of a whole new class of celestial objects, called active galaxies.

In advancing so far from the mere recording of loud and soft noises emanating from the stars, radio astronomers had gradually become impatient with their science's inability to offer its data in a readily comprehensible form. What they craved was a way of converting their data—typically multitudes of numbers representing variations in intensity—into pictures as readily comprehensible as those created in optical astronomy.

The first steps toward such a conversion were taken by Australian radio astronomers in the early 1950s. An L-shaped interferometer had been built near Sydney for the purpose of studying the Sun. It consisted of thirty-two small dishes laid out in a line, east to west; another sixteen antennas extended north and south. With this arrangement, the array could view the solar disk from many directions as the Earth rotated on its own axis and revolved around the Sun. Two Australian radiophysicists, Wilbur N. Christiansen and J. A. Warburton, recognized that the data they were collecting held the code to a radio "image" of the Sun—what would be seen by a creature with radio eyes.

Translating the code into a picture called for a laborious mathematical process known as the Fourier transform. In one version, the Fourier transform can reveal the basic components of complex phenomena; in another it can combine components into a whole. Christiansen and Warburton employed the second version to plot an image of the Sun's regions of radio brightness. This was the last time such a map was drawn for about ten years, mainly because it took the two radiophysicists half a year to perform the necessary Fourier calculations by hand. It was clear that a faster means of processing Fourier transforms was desperately needed.

FILLING IN THE DISH

As great a convenience as pictures of the radio sky might be, there was an even more compelling reason for speeding up calculations of Fourier transforms— increased resolution. Briefly, the principle is this: From the point of view of a radio source in space, paired radio telescopes appear to move closer together or farther apart as the Earth rotates. In effect, passing time causes them to occupy different points on the curved surface of the imaginary receiving dish that the two telescopes define—and more points, of course, mean greater resolution. The process of filling in the imaginary radio dish is called aperture synthesis. Accomplishing this legerdemain requires extensive use of Fourier transforms to combine, into a single radio image, the signals from multiple antennas throughout an observation period that might last several hours (pages 78-79).

Fourier transforms have broad application in science, and it happened that biochemists at Cambridge University were using the technique to unravel the structure of crystals just when an innovative Cambridge radio astronomer named Martin Ryle came up with the idea of aperture synthesis. To handle the complex calculations of X-ray crystallography, the biochemists had turned to computers, not only because the machines could perform calculations quickly, but also because they could use a variation of the transform that is possible only in binary mathematics, the computer's own language of ones and zeros. Called the fast Fourier transform, this variation gave even the relatively slow computers of the mid-1950s the capability of processing radio-telescope data quickly enough to make aperture synthesis practical.

In Ryle's scheme, the computer first stored data from all the observations by each pair of telescopes constituting the interferometer. Then the computer merged the signals, mimicking the radio waves coming to a common focus. Finally, it converted the myriad numbers into a picture of the radio object.

In 1958, Ryle and his colleagues began to test aperture synthesis by building the One-Mile Radio Telescope at the Mullard Radio Astronomy Laboratory, located outside Cambridge. Three dishes, each sixty feet in diameter, were placed along an east-west axis. The two end dishes were fixed; the middle one moved between them along a mile-long railroad track, pulled by a diesel tractor. By recording signals at many positions as the central antenna was moved (and the Earth rotated), this arrangement could sweep out an aperture a mile across. In one leap, Ryle made more than a twentyfold improvement in the resolution available to radio astronomers, achieving as fine a view of the heavens as that produced by an optical telescope with a four-inch reflector. The theory and practical application of aperture synthesis earned Ryle a Nobel Prize in 1974.

Synthetic-aperture arrays soon sprouted around the globe. At Westerbork in the Netherlands, Dutch astronomers constructed a fourteen-dish system that extended two miles; by 1972, Ryle had established a three-mile array, which consisted of eight dishes set in a row. With their improved vision, radio astronomers beheld a strange and wondrously new universe filled with galaxies whose primary radiation was radio energy.

Upon closer examination, these radio galaxies revealed a startling architectural feature. By combining the optical image of a radio galaxy with its radio-wave likeness, astronomers saw that the visible galaxies were only tiny smudges caught between giant lobes of gaseous matter. Looking like a pair of butterfly wings, the gaseous masses stretched for hundreds of thousands or even millions of light-years beyond the galaxy's luminous edge.

A comprehensive survey of the radio sky, undertaken by Ryle's group, turned up other celestial exotica—most notably small, extraordinarily powerful, and extremely distant radio sources, which, in photographs, looked like faint blue stars. Initially, all such objects were called quasi-stellar radio sources, or quasars. More recently, the name quasar has been reserved for an object that gives off more than 95 percent of its energy outside the visible spectrum. Today, quasars are believed to be newborn galaxies with very energetic nuclei. But in radio astronomy's infancy, they were a mystery. The desire to expose the "engines" powering these radio-bright objects spurred radio astronomers around the world to build even bigger interferometers. At the head of the pack was the National Radio Astronomy Observatory (NRAO) in the United States.

Established in the early 1950s by the National Science Foundation, the NRAO constructed its first radio telescope in 1959. The dish had a diameter of only eighty-five feet and resided in a picturesque valley in the Allegheny Mountains near Green Bank, West Virginia, an isolated region where cosmic radio waves could be gathered with little interference from the radio noises emitted by aircraft, automobiles, and television transmitters. Three years later, a 300-foot dish was added. By that time, however, astronomers at the NRAO had already formulated a concept for a synthetic-aperture array that would mimic a dish twenty miles in diameter. When completed, the array would match the resolution of the best optical telescopes—a goal that, for radio astronomers, was akin to climbing Mount Everest. Observatory planners dubbed their proposed interferometer the Very Large Array, or VLA.

The driving force behind America's entry into radio astronomy on a grand scale was David Heeschen, director of the NRAO. Heeschen had enrolled at the University of Illinois shortly after the end of World War II, with the intention of studying agriculture. But engineering and physics caught his fancy. When he attended Harvard University to pursue graduate work, Heeschen was coaxed into helping build a twenty-four-foot radio dish for the university observatory. "That's how I got into radio astronomy," he later recalled, "because I had a background in physics and knew some electronics." He was the first scientist to join the NRAO staff.

Heeschen saw the VLA, erected in stages, become fully operational in 1980. Its twenty-seven majestic white dishes, each measuring eighty-two feet across, are laid out in the shape of a Y in a dry lake bed on the Plains of San Augustin, in western New Mexico. Together, the dishes serve as radio astronomy's premier eye on the universe.

An important strength of the Very Large Array is its ability to act as a kind of giant zoom lens. Every few months, VLA technicians move the antennas along railroad tracks toward the center of the Y. In this configuration, each arm of the arrangement is no more than half a mile long. The result is a small aperture with relatively little resolving power but a broad view. In effect, it synthesizes the aperture of a wide-angle lens, allowing astronomers to study large fields of radio emission, such as wispy remnants of exploded stars. Then, to zoom in for a closer look at an object of interest, the antennas are stationed along the full length of the Y's arms—each about ten miles long. In this formation, the VLA approaches a 100-inch optical telescope in resolution and magnification.

TRAINING THE DISHES
The nerve center of the VLA is a two-story building situated near the crook of the Y. From a control room filled with display screens, computers monitor more than 200 different functions for each antenna. The most impressive feature of the room is the vast expanse of windows. They allow observers a splendid view of

Workers stop traffic as they maneuver a telescope of the twenty-seven-dish Very Large Array across a highway near Socorro, New Mexico. Every seven weeks, one of the parabolic antennas is taken to a maintenance building for routine repairs. For these moves and for changes in the array's configuration, the 215-ton telescopes travel on railroad tracks towed by tractors that roll alongside the rails. Together, the dishes—each ninety-two feet tall and eighty-two feet in diameter—simulate a telescope twenty miles across.

antenna choreography as the dishes turn in unison toward a new target in response to orders from the "Boss," the VLA's main computer.

To initiate an observation, an astronomer prepares a computer file that contains the name and position of the desired radio source, the time to start the observation, the time to stop it, and the radio wavelength to be collected, which can range from 1.3 to 90 centimeters. Astronomers can even transmit these instructions by telephone.

The Boss sends commands through a forty-mile-long network of two-inch, copper-lined, steel tubes buried beneath the lake bed. Such tubes are called wave guides; they can be used instead of wires where enormous amounts of data are to be carried for short distances. Cosmic radio transmissions, gathered by the dishes, are carried back to the computers by the same tubes. At the control center, these signals are amplified, digitized, and passed through circuitry that synchronizes data arriving from the far edge of the array with transmissions received from antennas closer in. A bank of special-purpose computers called correlators—isolated from spurious radio noises in a steel-lined room—then synthesize this data.

The VLA turned out to be so sensitive that high-quality radio maps of a strong source could be generated from an observation lasting only five minutes, rather than the eight to ten hours required by previous interferometers, which had fewer dishes to receive signals. Because the VLA is so fast, astronomers are tempted to take dozens of "snapshots" of their sources, placing a heavy burden on the telescope's data-processing system. When its dishes are on a target, the VLA collects 20,000 bits of data every second. Over a year's time, with the array operating nearly around the clock, almost 100 billion bits are accumulated. The production of images from the array's raw data requires far more computer time than dish-operating time. "The largest problem we have," VLA astronomer Barry Clark has said, "is that we don't have enough computers to keep up with all the data processing we would like to do." Given the VLA's capabilities, this shortcoming is likely to persist.

REFINING THE PICTURES

Like most complex computer applications, getting the VLA computers into operation was no simple task. For example, designing the software to interpret radio data from the stars and convert it into pictures was a job that took the equivalent of one programmer working thirty years. Knowing that the software was integral to the array's success and suspecting that writing it would entail a good bit of work, NRAO began developing the system at its headquarters in Charlottesville, Virginia, in 1978.

The result, completed more than two years later, was the Astronomical Image Processing System (AIPS), a software package that now includes about 600,000 lines of code. AIPS has become the world standard for observers constructing images from radio-telescope data. Maintained by a full-time staff of programmers located in Charlottesville, the code is updated every few months in order to accommodate new experiments that had not been foreseen when the original software was written.

A valued feature of AIPS is the program's ability to produce accurate pictures from incomplete information. Since there are always holes in an array—spaces without antennas—the initial pictures generated by the computer also have holes. Known as "dirty" images, they are grainy in appearance. A program within AIPS, called Clean, fills in the missing pieces. It works by calculating the most likely value for each hole from the values of its neighbors. The assumption behind the program is one of simple interpolation: A hole lying about a third of the distance between two known intensities, for example, should have an intensity about one-third of the way between them. The cost of this image enhancement is many hours of computing time. Other programs, even more computer-intensive, remove the errors introduced by the same atmospheric disturbances that cause stars to twinkle. Overall, a cleaned-up, filled-in image requires between 10 and 100 times as much computer time as a dirty image.

The additional processing can be well worth the effort, however. This was clearly the case when astronomers pursued their examinations of the radio galaxy Cygnus A. Earlier studies indicated that Cygnus A consists of two gigantic clouds of radio-emitting gas flanking a barely visible galactic center. Intense lines of radio energy appeared to pierce the galaxy. With the VLA, astronomers identified these lines as two streams of matter shooting from the galaxy's center toward the clouds of gas. These narrow cosmic jets, composed of charged particles traveling at very high speed, squirt across intergalactic space until they encounter an obstacle in the form of a gaseous region. There, somewhat like a powerful stream of water splashing against a brick wall, the charged particles fly off the obstacle to form winglike clouds. Astronomers now know that thousands of radio galaxies share the twin-jet design of Cygnus A.

A TELESCOPE AS BIG AS THE EARTH

Even with the keen vision of the Very Large Array, radio astronomers have been unable to solve some of the most intriguing cosmic riddles. For example, they need better resolution than the VLA's to explain the twin-jet phenomenon, though they suspect that the images they see are one of the shapes a galaxy takes when it contains a black hole. The answer very likely will come from interferometers whose antennas are positioned thousands of miles apart.

Linking dishes by cable or even by microwave radio links is impractically expensive over such distances. But as early as 1960, astronomers in the United States and Canada realized that, instead of establishing a direct connection, they could record the signals received at widely separated antennas on magnetic tape and then forward them to a central processing center for interpretation. Doing so would require synchronizing the replay of the tapes to within one quadrillionth of a second. Such precision is necessary to assure that the resulting picture of a radio source is based solely on data contributed by identical waves arriving at each antenna. This exquisite timing is made possible by a clock whose pendulum is the vibration of atoms in a crystal at the heart of the timepiece. Stationing such an atomic clock at each antenna guarantees that separate recordings can later be synchronized closely enough to produce sharp radio images.

The technique is called Very Long Baseline Interferometry (VLBI). First practiced in 1965, it has become a global enterprise. VLBI observers think of the process as 10 percent looking and 90 percent computing. A six-telescope session lasting twelve hours fills eighteen tapes with trillions of bits of raw data. VLBI investigators regularly borrow time on radio dishes scattered about North America and Europe. On occasion, radio telescopes in South America, Australia, the Soviet Union, and Japan are brought into the network. With such an intercontinental array, observers can create a radio antenna as wide as the Earth itself and attain resolutions 500 times sharper than the VLA. An optical telescope of comparable quality would offer the ability to read a newspaper in St. Louis from New York City.

VLBI is hindered by the variety of radio telescopes enlisted in the networks. During processing, computers must compensate for these differences in order to create an accurate image. To reduce the computing load—and thereby increase the number of observations made—a group of radio dishes dedicated to VLBI is being established across the United States. Labeled the Very Long Baseline Array, or VLBA, ten VLA-type antennas are to be located at sites in Hawaii, Washington, California, Arizona, New Mexico, Iowa, Texas, New Hampshire, Massachusetts, and St. Croix. A master computer in New Mexico, near the Very Large Array, will orchestrate the movements of each dish through messages sent over telephone lines. The network will stretch into space when a VLBI antenna is sent into Earth orbit, sometime in the 1990s. Then, astronomers may get their first glimpse of the dynamos lurking at the center of radio galaxies.

X-RAY SECRETS

Among the many marvels harvested from the skies by radio astronomy are neutron stars—star relics that weigh billions of tons per cubic inch and often send out regular radio pulses as they rotate. The intense radio signals that emanate

Two views of radio galaxy Cygnus A illustrate the benefits of image enhancement by computer. Before processing (below), the bright nucleus of the galaxy appears to be unrelated to the globular masses in the corners. After the image data is passed through computer programs called Clean and Maximum Entropy, the nucleus is revealed to be the source of two so-called jets, high-speed emanations of matter that form clouds when they collide with cooler, denser matter nearer the galaxy's edge.

from such strange objects imply temperatures and energy levels far beyond the scope of human experience—the same conditions from which very-high-energy radiations, such as X rays, would also be expected to pour forth.

From the earliest days of radio astronomy, some scientists had suspected that X rays might figure importantly in the processes behind the turbulent universe. Working for the Naval Research Laboratory (NRL) on communications problems similar to those that Karl Jansky studied, Edward Hulbert theorized in 1938 that X rays emanate from the Sun. But proof seemed unattainable. Although they penetrate flesh and concrete, X rays are absorbed by the oxygen and nitrogen in the Earth's atmosphere. Even weather balloons, rising to a height of twenty-five miles or so, could not reach the altitudes where this presumptive radiation might be detected. X-ray astronomy awaited the development of rockets that could escape the atmosphere altogether.

The first of these were V-2 missiles confiscated from the Germans after World War II. In 1948, researchers at the NRL sent aloft a piece of film in a lightproof container. When recovered after the flight, the film was fogged, suggesting that Hulbert was right about the Sun's production of X rays. A sheet of film, however, is no substitute for a telescope. Fully thirty years would pass before such a device was built, in part because most X rays are absorbed when they hit a mirror and cannot be easily focused.

In the meantime, astronomers had to content themselves with modified Geiger counters—instruments known for their use in uranium prospecting—that detected the presence of X rays and gave a rough measure of intensity. Physicist Herbert Friedman, who joined NRL in 1940, made the modifications by filling

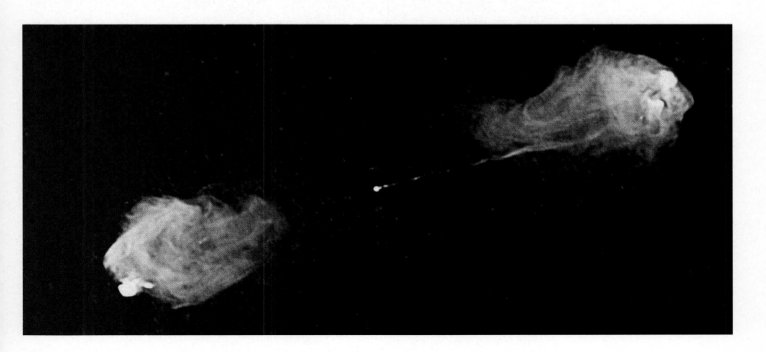

Views of the Invisible

Radio astronomers rely on a panoply of computer-graphics techniques to convert invisible details of the universe into images that can be seen and measured. To produce a portrait of a radio source in space, a computer begins with intensities of radio emissions collected by a radio-telescope system. The full range of radio intensities, from the faint background noise that permeates space to the strongest signal in the sky, is divided into increments called brightness levels. Each is assigned a number and stored, along with its location, in a data base. The amount of information in the data base is prodigious—typically hundreds of megabytes of intensity information assigned to several thousand brightness levels.

Instead of converting all this information into an image, which would be too costly in computer time and would overwhelm a viewer with detail, an astronomer instructs the computer to select perhaps as few as ten evenly spaced brightness levels to work with. The computer converts each intensity in the data base to the nearest of the ten levels and assigns the number to a grid, the squares of which represent the locations of picture elements, or pixels, of a computer monitor. The center section of such a grid appears below.

The intensity of each pixel having been established, an astronomer has several options for displaying the information. The computer can convert the numbers in the grid into shades of gray, ranging from black to white. A contour map can be produced, with lines joining grid squares sharing the same value. Or the numbers can be rendered as peaks and valleys.

The astronomer can call for an image that shows a broad view of the subject or can ask the computer to zoom in close, as in the examples at right. The subject of these images, which cover about 100,000 light-years measured diagonally, is the radio galaxy NGC 326, as observed by the Very Large Array in New Mexico (*pages 80-81*). NGC 326 has a brilliant radio center from which rush, in opposite directions, jets of matter that emit radio signals about half as strong as those coming from the core.

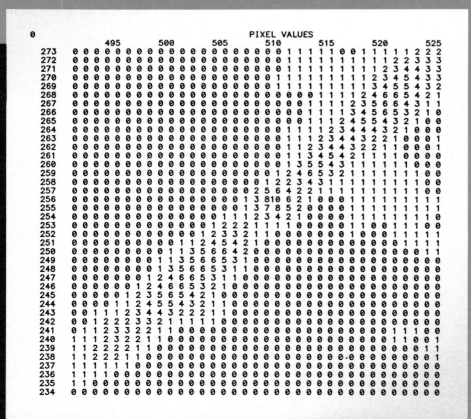

A section of the grid. More than a thousand brightness values reveal the intensity of radio emissions from NGC 326. The range of intensities has been divided into ten equal steps, with zero assigned to the radio background noise that is found everywhere in the cosmos and ten representing the strongest emissions intercepted from the galaxy. A pattern emerges from the numbers that hints at the shape of the galaxy—made clearer in the renditions at right. Numbers along the top and left side of the grid at left are coordinates for a computer screen having a total of 524,288 pixels, 1,024 horizontally and 512 vertically.

A rendering in grays. The energetic nucleus of NGC 326 and the galaxy's jets are readily visible in a gray-scale display. This image, which somewhat resembles a crude photograph, was produced by instructing the computer to convert each brightness value in the data base into one of 256 shades of gray from minimum intensity (white, or zero) to black. Astronomers use gray-scale images not only to have a first look at a radio source, but to spot subtle patterns in areas of background noise where any hint of structure suggests that something may have gone awry with the computer processing that created the image.

A contour map. Lines in this view of NGC 326 join points of equal radio-emission intensity, as contour lines on a topographical map link points of equal height. Contour-map software uses a process called interpolation to draw line segments between squares in the grid. Though time-consuming, the method produces a picture of the galaxy from which accurate measurements can be taken. For example, by comparing the width of a jet near the galaxy nucleus with the jet's width thousands of light-years away, astronomers can judge the density of gases surrounding the galaxy at various distances from the center.

Seeing the peaks and valleys. This type of image, called a ruled-surface plot, gives a solid, three-dimensional impression of the radio galaxy. Though shown for a relatively small area, it is most helpful to an astronomer in cataloging all the radio emitters in a large region of space. Even point sources of radio emissions, which might be lost in both the gray-scale and contour-map views, stand out clearly in a ruled-surface plot.

a sealed steel box with a gas, usually argon. One side had a penny-size aperture covered with foil of a thickness that would let X rays pass but would block other wavelengths. A positively charged wire in the box was meant to attract energetic particles. When an X ray penetrated the foil and struck an atom of argon, the collision dislodged an electron from the gas. The freed electron was attracted by the positively charged wire; speeding in that direction, it knocked additional electrons loose from other argon atoms. As electrons hit the wire, they produced an electrical current having a strength corresponding to the energy of the incoming X rays.

These proportional Geiger counters, as they were called, could not produce images; they could merely indicate the strength of an X-ray signal and the direction from which the signal came. Friedman sent such a detector into space on a V-2 rocket in September 1949. At an altitude of seventy miles or so, the detector registered a strong signal when it was pointed toward the Sun, proving Hulbert's hypothesis.

Friedman and his colleagues dominated X-ray astronomy throughout the 1950s and developed many of its tools. Using the Aerobee research rocket, the NRL team examined solar X-ray emissions over an entire eleven-year sunspot cycle. Computers were vital in working out rocket trajectories, but they played no role in data gathering at this stage. "We could look at the record radioed down from the detector," recalls Friedman, "and lay out the whole set of results in ten or fifteen minutes."

RISKY ASTRONOMY
Other astronomers hesitated to join the new endeavor because the the field was unpredictable: Rockets blew up and experiments were lost. Furthermore, extrapolating from Friedman's solar measurements, theorists figured that X-ray emissions from faraway stars and galaxies would be minuscule, too weak to warrant special study. However, a few bold pioneers—in particular, a physicist named Riccardo Giacconi—believed otherwise.

Born in Italy in 1931, Giacconi grew up with a passion for architecture, but he was doubtful of his artistic abilities and chose instead to study physics. Arriving in the United States on a Fulbright scholarship when he was twenty-five years old, he went first to Indiana University and then to Princeton to conduct research on cosmic rays—charged particles that continually bombard the Earth from interstellar space. In 1959, he was hired by American Science and Engineering, Inc. (AS&E), a NASA and military contractor based in Massachusetts, to set up a program in space science.

A fortuitous meeting shortly thereafter established Giacconi's agenda for the next twenty years. At a social gathering, he was introduced to Bruno Rossi, an Italian-born physicist who was noted for his work with cosmic rays. Rossi was convinced that major new discoveries were in the offing for those investigating high-energy radiation, and he recommended that Giacconi pursue X-ray astronomy. According to Giacconi, who for months had been searching for a suitable space-science project, Rossi's tip "was a seminal suggestion, which all of a sudden gave me a way to go." Giacconi became, as he described it, "a man possessed."

Shortly after their encounter, Giacconi and Rossi published a paper that predicted the likely types of X-ray sources—the chaotic remains of supernova explosions, for example, or the flares that shoot forth from very hot stars. Giacconi then began his X-ray hunt by working to improve proportional counters—specifically, giving them greater powers of discrimination. The problem was that the devices reacted to cosmic rays and X rays as if they were the same. This was of no great consequence when examining the Sun, because solar X rays outnumber solar cosmic rays by a million to one. But since the ultimate goal of the AS&E scientists was to look beyond the sun for sources of X rays, they had to find a way of avoiding such misidentification. The higher energy of cosmic rays provided an answer. While X rays are absorbed by the gas inside an X-ray detector, cosmic rays shoot right through the instrument. To ensure that X rays and cosmic rays could be distinguished, Giacconi simply surrounded a proportional X-ray counter with an additional detector. Any signal produced in both detectors was discarded. Every signal that produced a single response was an X ray.

AS&E persuaded the U.S. Air Force to launch three of Giacconi's improved counters into space aboard an air force research shot. On June 18, 1962, at one minute before midnight, an Aerobee rocket streaked skyward from the White Sands Missile Range in southern New Mexico carrying the trio of instruments. A scant 350 seconds later, as planned, the rocket plunged back to Earth.

Those six minutes were exceedingly productive. The detectors recorded a huge flux of X rays from the direction of the constellation Scorpius. The short-wavelength radiation blazed with an intensity beyond anyone's imagination, billions of times greater than the Sun's X-ray output. The mysterious source was labeled Sco X-1.

In early 1963, detectors aboard another Aerobee research flight—this one conducted for Herbert Friedman and his colleagues at NRL—confirmed the sighting and also snared X rays emanating from a famous supernova remnant, the Crab nebula. Over the ensuing years, both the NRL and AS&E researchers sought to find additional X-ray objects. "By 1964, we produced a catalog of some three dozen sources," recalls Friedman. Yet a comprehensive survey would require decades to complete if rockets had to be used for all observation. Astronomers in this field needed a way to probe space for lengthy periods.

PROGRAMMING *UHURU*

Within a year and a half of the Sco X-1 discovery, Giacconi presented NASA with a bold, long-range plan for X-ray astronomy. He wanted to develop an "X-ray explorer" satellite with the longevity to make a detailed survey of the entire sky. The project was approved by NASA in 1966, and construction of the satellite's scientific payload was entrusted to AS&E. Work got under way in converted milk-truck garages in Cambridge, Massachusetts.

Computers were slated for critical roles. For example, "there would have been no way to know where the satellite was pointed without computers," says Ethan Schreier, a theoretical physicist who signed on at AS&E to support his graduate education and stayed to become a pioneer in the application of computers to space astronomy. Satellites are disturbed in orbit by a variety of forces, such as small variations in the Earth's gravity or occasional "kicks" from the planet's magnetic field. To pinpoint X-ray sources in the heavens, it would be necessary to always know the satellite's exact position and orientation—its aspect, in aerospace parlance. Schreier, who became known as Mr. Aspect because of the assignment, planned to have a computer perform this task by comparing patterns of stars detected by optical telescopes aboard the satellite with a computerized star catalog on Earth.

Computers would also be vital for data processing. During preflight testing of the X-ray satellite, AS&E brought PDP-11 minicomputers, developed by the Digital Equipment Corporation, into their laboratories. Much faster than the computers they replaced, the PDP-11s permitted a switch from processing the satellite data in batches collected over a period of time to handling the information the instant it became available. To Schreier, this switch from the delays of batch processing to real-time computing was revolutionary. "In astronomy," he explains, "it's so important, when seeing an image of the data, to be able to say, 'I'd like to change that parameter a bit,' and then view the results while you're still sitting there. This was a very big change for us."

AN ORBITING TELESCOPE

After some four years of designing, building, testing, and adjusting, AS&E's X-ray astronomy satellite was launched from a modified oil-drilling rig off the coast of Kenya on that country's Independence Day, December 12, 1970. The site was chosen because a rocket launched at the equator gets a maximum boost in speed from the Earth's rotation. The trajectory also bypasses the Van Allen radiation belt. Giacconi feared that highly charged particles trapped by the Earth's atmosphere in these belts would throw off readings of the proportional counters. Officially labeled the Small Astronomy Satellite-1, the observatory was immediately named *Uhuru*—the Swahili word for freedom—in honor of Kenya's seventh anniversary of independence.

Uhuru's proportional counters worked flawlessly, registering where the sky was bright in X rays and where it was dark. Each second, the detectors generated 1,000 bits of data, which was transmitted to the NASA Goddard Space Flight Center in Maryland and then to AS&E headquarters over telephone lines. The satellite inspected a different swath of sky—five degrees long and one degree wide—each day.

Positioning of the satellite—worked out by a Goddard computer—was done by sending a carefully calibrated amount of current through magnetic coils aboard *Uhuru;* this current interacted with the Earth's magnetic field to move *Uhuru* ever so slightly. Six months were required to cover the entire celestial sphere; then another set of observations began, planned so that each sector would be scanned again from a different direction. Sources of X-ray radiation became more clearly defined as *Uhuru* investigators overlaid the results of multiple scans of a region.

In most instances, the data radioed to Earth from the *Uhuru* detectors followed a pattern that had been anticipated: The signal intensity from an X-ray source would first rise, then fall, as the satellite, spinning sedately at one revolution every twelve minutes, turned the counters toward the source, then away from it. But inspection of the data as it came in indicated that some of the responses were not perfectly regular. At times, "bumps" in signal intensity appeared, revealing a component of signal-intensity fluctuation that could not be accounted for by the satellite's rotation. The only possible cause of the phenomenon was that these

A Scout rocket blasts off from an oil-drilling platform near the coast of Kenya on December 12, 1970, lifting the X-ray satellite *Uhuru* into orbit 500 miles above the Earth. The equatorial launch site was chosen to give maximum advantage from the Earth's rotation. Over the next four years the NASA research satellite reaped a rich harvest of X-ray views of the cosmos.

X-ray emissions varied in strength. The burning question was whether these pulsations were periodic or random.

Cen X-3, the third strongest source in the Centaurus constellation and one displaying prominent bumps, provided the answer. Giacconi and his team spent days studying this single source. By slowing the satellite's spin, the AS&E scientists were able to stretch out the signal for a better look. But since *Uhuru's* spin could not be stopped entirely without destabilizing the satellite, Ethan Schreier had to write a computer program that would be able to follow the phases of Cen X-3's pulsations from one sighting to the next—"a tour de force in computing," says Giacconi.

Schreier's software revealed that every 4.8 seconds the X-ray intensity would rise sharply, then fall. After months of observation, astronomers realized that the interval between these pulsations increased and decreased according to a repeating schedule. This performance proved, for the same reason that a train whistle rises in pitch when the train approaches and falls after it passes, that Cen X-3 raced toward the Earth at regular intervals, then rushed away, as if it were orbiting another object.

The hypothesis was confirmed by another observation: Every two days, for a dozen hours, the pulses would disappear. In astronomy, such conduct is a sure sign of an eclipse, that is, one object passing from view behind another. There was no doubt that Cen X-3 formed half of a double-star system. X rays from the pulsar were regularly blocked as Cen X-3 orbited a nearby stellar companion that emitted no X rays. *Uhuru* had discovered a whole new class of celestial objects: X-ray binaries. Cen X-3, with its smoothly varying changes in the frequency of the X-ray pulses, was revealed as a neutron star in orbit around a giant companion.

Other X-ray sources are not as periodic as Cen X-3. For example, Cygnus X-1, another prominent fountain of X rays, displayed no regularity in its flare-ups. Sometimes, the sporadic flickers were as short as fractions of a second. *Uhuru's* scientists were determined to find out why.

The first clue came from clever detective work by radio and optical astronomers that showed Cygnus X-1 was orbiting around a giant blue star companion. They also determined that Cygnus X-1 weighed far more than a neutron star, making it appear suspiciously like a black hole—a massive star that, at the end of its life, had collapsed into oblivion, creating a gravitational field so intense that no bit of light or matter can escape. The conclusion: Cygnus X-1 is probably pulling gas away from its blue companion. As the gas approaches Cygnus X-1, it begins erratically emitting X rays while swirling down the space-time drain.

AN X-RAY TELESCOPE

Uhuru transmitted data for four years. By the time of its demise, hundreds of X-ray sources were cataloged. Meanwhile, Giacconi nurtured a larger dream: He wanted to develop a telescope that could actually focus on X-ray sources. Inasmuch as X rays have much shorter wavelengths than visible light, he hoped to achieve high resolving power in an instrument much smaller than a comparable optical telescope. The path to such an instrument had been charted by Hans Wolter, a German physicist who attempted in the late 1940s to find a means of focusing X rays for use as an X-ray microscope.

Wolter realized that X rays could be focused by reflection only if they struck a mirror at a so-called grazing angle of less than one degree, like bullets ricocheting off a wall. The best images would form, he figured, if X rays were reflected twice, first from a shallow paraboloid mirror and second from a shallow hyperboloid reflector that would focus the final image.

Wolter was forced to abandon his microscope because he found it too difficult to make small mirrors of adequate precision, but Giacconi saw that Wolter's design could work effectively on the larger scale of a telescope. In fact, he had tried—unsuccessfully—to interest NASA in developmental work back in 1960. At the time, Giacconi proposed a tapered cylinder with a parabolically shaped inner surface near the entrance at the wide end. Deeper inside the cylinder, the sides would become hyperboloid. When Giacconi described his plan to Bruno Rossi, his colleague pointed out that more X rays could be gathered—and a brighter image produced—if several such telescopes were nested one inside the other.

This time, NASA was interested, but the space agency wanted the X-ray telescopes for solar astronomy rather than stellar research. In a joint venture,

AS&E engineers collaborated with their counterparts at the Goddard Space Center to design a simple telescope, less than a yard long, three inches wide, and resembling a mailing tube. Two of the X-ray telescopes—one in 1963 and one in 1965—were rocketed above the atmosphere and successfully obtained pictures of the Sun on film. Improved versions of these telescopes flew aboard NASA's Skylab space station in 1973, enabling astronauts to take thousands of X-ray pictures of the Sun. The instruments produced views that equaled the resolution of a small optical reflector.

The spectacular Skylab images, coupled with *Uhuru*'s tremendous finds, finally tipped the scales in favor of a telescope devoted to studies of X-ray objects outside the Solar System: After years of lobbying, Giacconi got the go-ahead in 1973 to construct a large focusing X-ray telescope for NASA's High Energy Astronomy Observatory (HEAO) program. At about this time, Giacconi moved into the Harvard-Smithsonian Center for Astrophysics, taking several of his colleagues with him. AS&E had found it increasingly difficult to maintain a high-level research branch, and the Center for Astrophysics on the nearby Harvard campus beckoned with laboratory space and funding. There, developmental work proceeded.

THE EINSTEIN OBSERVATORY
Giacconi and his colleagues wanted an instrument that could view sources a thousand times fainter than those revealed by proportional counters and would equal the best radio telescopes in resolution. To get it, they needed a complex of instruments; no single detector could make detailed X-ray images, take in a large field, and also show sensitivity to weak sources. They decided to incorporate four kinds of detectors into a single telescope.

Two sets of concentric mirrors—parabolas first, followed by hyperbolas—reflect X rays toward a common focus in this diagram of the Einstein X-ray telescope. Rays entering the telescope strike the reflectors at a shallow angle so that they are not absorbed by the mirrors. The telescope's total reflective surface—and hence sensitivity—is maximized by the nesting of mirrors one inside another.

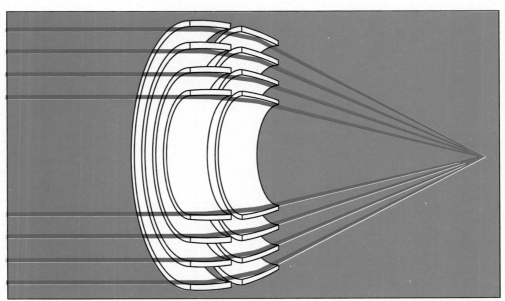

Each detector was a highly polished, nickel-coated glass cylinder with an outside diameter of nearly two feet. These big tubes were mounted on a turntable so that the desired detector could be rotated into use as it was needed. Two of the detectors measured the strength of X-ray wavelengths emitted by a source. The remaining two made images of the targets. One of them, the Imaging Proportional Counter, provided a broad view, about as sharp as the image that would be seen by the human eye. The other, called the High Resolution Imager, went after far more detail.

The High Resolution Imager posed the greatest technical challenge because nothing like it had been built before. Since film could not be retrieved from an unmanned satellite, an electronic X-ray-imaging camera had to be devised. To

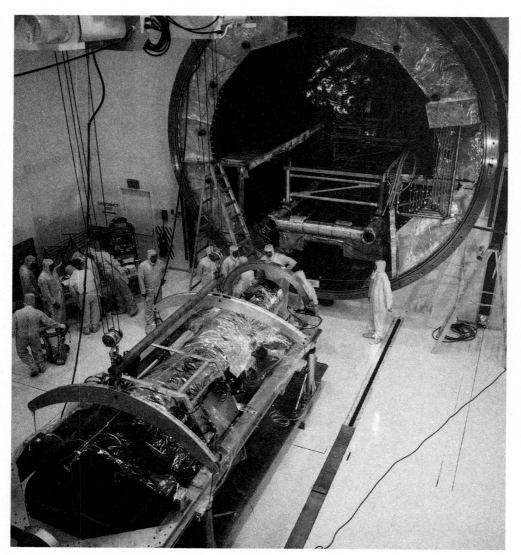

Technicians dressed in clean-room garb hover around the Einstein X-ray telescope, nestled in a cradle outside a vacuum chamber at the Marshall Space Flight Center in Huntsville, Alabama. A plastic shroud protects the satellite from dirt and debris that could fall from the overhead hoist used to lift the telescope into the chamber, where it is tested under conditions that simulate the vacuum of space.

do this, Giacconi's team borrowed an X-ray detector, developed in England, called a microchannel plate.

The device consisted of an array of millions of tiny, specially coated glass tubes. Every strike by an X ray would release a cascade of electrons from the coating. The stronger the radiation, the greater the number of electrons released. After traveling down the tubes, the electrons fell onto a wire grid where they generated a signal. The strength of the pulse and its location on the grid were recorded and transmitted to Earth. A computer on the ground could then reconstruct a two-dimensional image of the source.

Planning the data analysis for the new telescope began in 1974, more than three years before the observatory would actually be launched. Computers touched every area of preparation—from generating the observation schedule to conducting a mock mission.

In the summer of 1977, the entire observatory was transported to the Marshall Space Flight Center in Huntsville, Alabama; final calibrations were to be tested in a vacuum chamber that simulated conditions in space. Concerned that the project was months behind schedule, NASA ordered six months of experiments, 1,397 tests in all, to be completed in just thirty days. The crash effort, performed around the clock, was successful mainly because the computer programs were able to analyze results immediately.

Shortly after midnight on November 13, 1978, the X-ray telescope was lofted into orbit aboard an Atlas-Centaur rocket launched from the Kennedy Space Center in Florida. The observatory was dubbed Einstein to honor the 1979 centennial of the scientist's birth. Astronomers chose X-ray astronomy's most notorious subject, Cygnus X-1, for their first target.

At "first light," the instant when a new telescope is turned on, Giacconi and his colleagues watched from Earth as the picture unfolded. As the source came into view, the team knew that they had built a working machine. Giacconi described it "as one of those joyful, almost intoxicating moments that occur all too seldom in a scientific career."

For two and a half years, until the orbiting observatory ran out of the precious fuel needed for the thruster rockets that were used to aim the X-ray telescope by reorienting the satellite, data was transmitted to NASA ground stations and then relayed to mission headquarters at the Harvard-Smithsonian Center for Astrophysics. Each month, based on a pool of acceptable proposals, a schedule of observations was generated at the Goddard Space Flight Center by means of software known as the Detailed Observing Program. Commands to carry out the computed sequence—target, choice of detector, and observing time— were radioed to the Einstein satellite every twelve hours. At the Center for Astrophysics, one computer processed the raw data and handled ongoing mission planning; another computer was available to astronomers for analysis and color image processing. The Einstein satellite was a national facility open to hundreds of guest observers, so other research groups had no need to launch their own detectors.

More than 7,000 images of the X-ray universe were collected by the Einstein telescope—pictures that will continue to be analyzed for years to come. The objects studied ranged from comets within the Solar System to the most distant galaxies. The observatory proved all stars to be X-ray sources at one level or another. It allowed identification of thousands of so-called active galaxies—prodigious emitters of energy.

The satellite established that, although quasars were discovered by radio telescope, more than 90 percent of them produce more X rays than radio waves. So many quasars were found that they became the explanation for a cosmic conundrum—a kind of background hum of X rays detected everywhere in the sky. This sea of X rays was identified as the collective output of billions of individual quasars, glowing too faintly in the visible or radio spectrums to be seen by optical or radio telescopes. The Einstein telescope also produced evidence that the power plant of a quasar may be a supermassive black hole, and it revealed the distribution patterns of a hot, X-ray-emitting gas that fills galaxy clusters. The gas, which is concentrated in the centers of some clusters and evenly dispersed in others, may be a key to understanding how galaxy families evolve.

With the Einstein observatory, X-ray astronomy joined its sister astronomies as an equal partner. For optical astronomy, the progression from Galileo's hand-held telescope to the enormous mirror on top of California's Mount Palomar—a millionfold increase in sensitivity—took more than three centuries. X-ray astronomers achieved similar improvements in sensitivity and resolution in less than two decades.

Radio Eyes on the Sky

Collecting radio waves. The parabolic shape of a radio-telescope dish reflects incoming radio waves toward a central focus, known as the subreflector *(red)*, which in turn directs the focused waves to a horn-shaped collector *(yellow)* in the dish's center. The waves are then converted into an electric current and forwarded via cable *(orange)* to a control room, where computers process and analyze the signals.

The radio portion of the electromagnetic spectrum has proved almost as bountiful for astronomy as it has in the realm of communications. And just as the simple "wireless" led directly to the sophisticated imaging technology of television, the crude antennas that first listened to the radio emissions of the cosmos in the 1930s rapidly evolved into instruments that can create extraordinarily detailed pictures of the sky—pictures full of information unattainable by even the most powerful optical telescopes.

Computers are essential to the process of extracting the meaning of celestial radio waves. Once the cosmic signals are gathered and focused by giant parabolic dishes *(left)*, they are converted first into a varying electric current and then into discrete digital pulses to be processed and analyzed by computers. Special algorithms take care of translating these signals into images equivalent to those produced quite naturally by optical telescopes. Computers also play an integral role in controlling the radio telescopes themselves, keeping them aimed at a selected target for the many hours needed for most radio observations.

As explained on the following pages, advances in computer technology have helped to overcome some of the inherent limitations of radio telescopes. Increasingly powerful computers now permit radio astronomers to quest for cosmic quarry far smaller than the best-equipped optical observers could hope to snare.

How a Single Dish Sees

Single-dish radio telescopes provide a whole new range of data about celestial objects, but in one regard they are less revealing than their optical counterparts: They are not nearly as effective at resolving fine detail in the objects they focus upon. The radio image at left of Galaxy NGC 326, for example, gives only a fuzzy view of the source of that galaxy's radio emissions. The blurring stems from a basic principle that affects all types of telescopes: In order to resolve images sharply, a telescope's aperture, or the diameter of its collecting area, must be many times greater than the wavelength of the radiation it detects. Because radio waves are, relatively speaking, very long from crest to crest, even large radio dishes have a tendency to produce fuzzy pictures.

The way in which a radio telescope collects waves helps explain how aperture size affects focusing ability. As the drawings on these two pages illustrate, the signal recorded by a radio dish is actually produced by the overlapping of waves reflected from pairs of points all over the dish's curved surface—a process that boosts the intensity of the signal wherever wave crests intersect. The telescope's resolution is determined by the width of the overlap of waves reflected from the outermost points on the dish. The farther apart these points are, the greater the angle at which the waves will intersect, which means crests will coincide only briefly, generating narrow bands of signal intensity and thus a more sharply focused final image. In a smaller dish, whose outer points would be closer together, the angle of intersection would be smaller, causing a broader portion of each crest to overlap and the recorded signal would be more diffuse, or fuzzier.

Patterns of interference. The six diagrams above show what happens when a radio wave from a distant astronomical source strikes the curved surface of a radio-telescope dish. Starting at the dish's outer edge, pairs of points equidistant from the center reflect secondary waves that interfere with each other as they radiate toward the telescope's focal plane *(red line)*, creating a pattern of signal intensity represented below each diagram as alternating bright and dark bands; where wave crests intersect *(green dots)*, the signal is reinforced, while between crests the waves cancel each other out and the signal is dampened. The bands of intensity widen as points progressively nearer the center reflect the incoming wave, producing fewer but broader inter-sections. As illustrated at right, the signal ultimately recorded at the telescope's focus is a single, brighter band *(bottom)* that results from the accumulation, or adding together, of all the pat-terns'· central bands; its width matches that of the narrowest central band because only that much of the signal is reinforced by every interference pattern. Only six patterns are shown here, but the actual signal would combine interference patterns from myriad pairs of points covering the dish's entire surface.

Improving the
View with Two Dishes

Although radio-based images get sharper as telescopes get larger, a single dish would have to be many miles across to achieve the resolution of an optical telescope with an aperture of only a few feet. Fortunately, radio astronomers are able to resolve more detail in their views of celestial objects by simulating such impossibly wide dishes electronically. The technique they use—interferometry—involves combining signals detected by two separate dishes, known together as an interferometer, whose distance apart defines the measure of the simulated dish's aperture.

Computers are the secret to the success of this electronic wizardry. They mimic the natural process of wave interference that occurs at the focal plane of an actual dish, simulating the rebounding of waves from paired points on a parabolic surface by the manner in which they process the recorded signals from two separate dishes. In addition, computers employ such techniques as Earth-rotation aperture synthesis (opposite) to fill in more pairs of points on the imaginary dish's surface.

Careful aiming of the dishes and timing of their signals (right) are also among the processing chores computers must perform to achieve precise simulations. The end result is a less blurred image, richer in detail. The view of NGC 326 shown here, for example, reveals two gaseous regions emanating from the galaxy's center that were barely distinguishable in the ne dish image.

Simulating a large dish. With the help of computer processing, two separate dishes can be made to act like points on the surface of a larger dish with greater resolving power. First, a computer synchronizes the arrival of incoming waves at both dishes by delaying the signal from one of them (above, left). Then it combines the output from both dishes in such a way as to simulate the interference pattern that would result if the waves were actually reflecting toward an imaginary focus. Finally, the simulated pattern (top bar) is merged with the signal from one of the dishes (middle) to produce a nar-

Adding more points. An even finer resolution can be achieved with two dishes by making use of the Earth's rotation to simulate more points on an imaginary dish. The aperture of the simulated dish is defined by the distance between the two real dishes when they are horizontally aligned relative to the radio source; from the perspective of the source, the two dishes then seem to move closer together as the Earth rotates *(top)*. By continuously combining the signals from the paired dishes over several hours, the computer in effect gathers data from a series of points on the simulated dish *(right)* and ends up with a tighter band of signal intensity *(above)*.

Harnessing the Power of Multiple Dishes

As computers have become more adept at managing complex systems, radio astronomers have been able to make major strides in the electronic simulation of telescope dishes. In Socorro, New Mexico, a collection of twenty-seven dishes known as the Very Large Array (VLA) duplicates the image-resolving power of a single dish up to twenty miles across, providing radio pictures of unrivaled quality and clarity; seen by the VLA, the two plasma plumes of NGC 326 appear in stunning detail *(above)*.

The processing tasks of such a system are legion. Computers must carefully coordinate the tracking movements of all twenty-seven dishes and synchronize signal reception to compensate for slight but significant differences in the distance between each dish and the celestial source. Only then can the intricate work of combining and analyzing the signals from every element in the array begin.

The VLA employs the same techniques of signal combination used when two dishes are linked, but while a single pair can represent at best only a few points on an imaginary dish *(page 79)*, the VLA's dishes can simulate almost an entire dish surface *(opposite)*. Each dish in the array is individually connected with every other dish to form hundreds of different interferometer pairings. The interference pattern generated by each pair as their signals are combined is fed to a computerized device called a correlator, which electronically merges these multiple patterns as if they were accumulating at the focus of an actual dish. In effect, all the physical processes of wave intersection and reinforcement that would occur in a real dish take place within the circuitry of computers.

An abundance of telescope pairs. The twenty-seven dishes of the Very Large Array (VLA) work in pairs to synthesize an aperture whose radius equals the length of each of the array's three arms. In the diagram above, black lines denote the connections between one dish—the outer one on the right-hand arm—and each of the other twenty-six dishes. In reality, every dish is similarly linked with all the others, creating a total of 351 individual pairings. Computers consolidate the data generated by each pair to produce an image.

Filling in the dish. Each of the VLA's 351 interferometer pairs contributes a different piece of information about a source just as pairs of points on a real dish would. As the Earth rotates and the positions of the dishes change, computers are able to collect data from a series of points that together cover almost the entire surface of the simulated dish, as represented by the curved tracings at left. The aperture dimensions vary, depending on the source's position in the sky; when dish pairs align vertically relative to a source near the horizon, they appear to be closer together than they would if the source were higher in the sky, and the simulated dish becomes more elongated (inset).

A Dish as
Large as the Earth

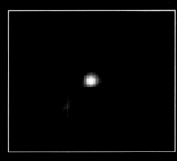

Computer prowess makes it possible not only to turn a group of relatively nearby telescopes into a single functioning unit but also to unite dishes scattered widely over the face of the Earth. The effect is akin to training a giant zoom lens on the heavens. The image here of NGC 326 represents a tight focus on the very heart of that galaxy, at a spot about midway between the two large plumes that were the predominant features of previous views.

As with less extensive interferometry systems, individual dishes are treated as pairs, and their signals are combined to create interference patterns that reflect the length of their baselines, or the distance between them. On a global scale, however, when partnered dishes may be separated by thousands of miles, alterations in computing strategy are called for. Each dish's signals are separately recorded on magnetic tape along with reference signals produced by atomic clocks accurate to an infinitesimal fraction of a second. The tapes are then flown to a central processing facility where computers synchronize the readings based on the reference signals. The computers may also have to compensate for signal anomalies caused by differences in dish sizes or recording methods or the effects of atmospheric distortion *(right)*. Finally, complex algorithms take care of combining the data in just the right way to duplicate the resolving power of an Earth-size dish.

A global array. Radio dishes linked in a worldwide network form interferometer pairs with baselines *(black lines)* ranging from hundreds to thousands of miles long. Because of the Earth's curvature, one dish of a pair may see a source directly overhead while the other sees it near the horizon. As a result, waves reaching the first dish travel a straight path through a minimum amount of atmosphere *(lower green arrow)*, while those headed for the second dish strike the atmosphere at an angle and are refracted *(upper arrow)*, following an altered course and encountering more of the Earth's distorting atmosphere. Computers must take these differences into account when they combine the two dishes' signals.

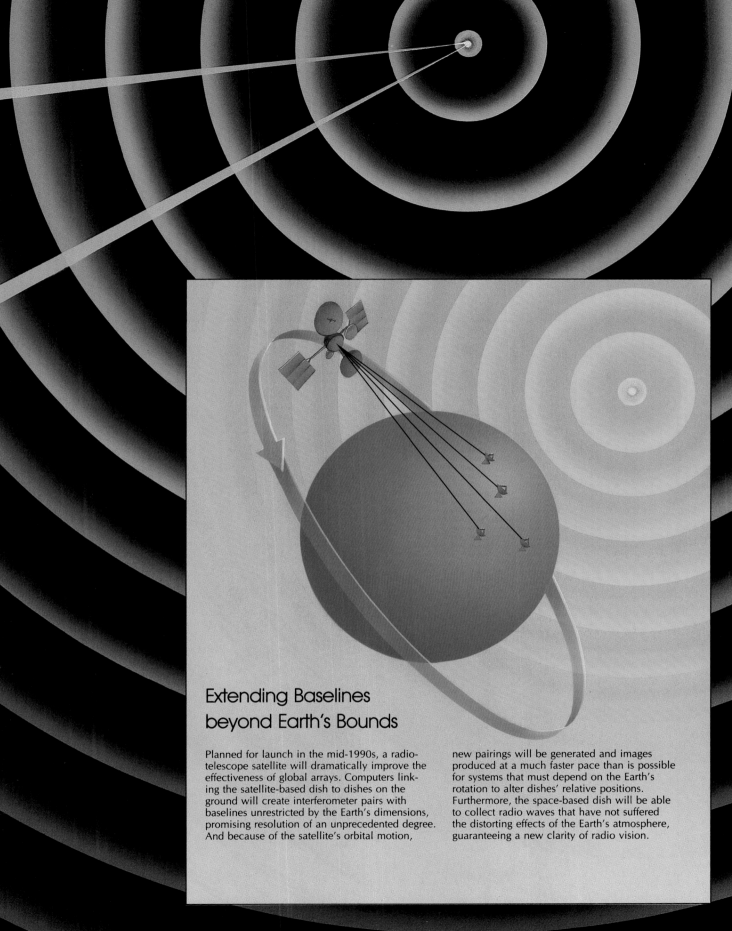

Extending Baselines
beyond Earth's Bounds

Planned for launch in the mid-1990s, a radio-telescope satellite will dramatically improve the effectiveness of global arrays. Computers linking the satellite-based dish to dishes on the ground will create interferometer pairs with baselines unrestricted by the Earth's dimensions, promising resolution of an unprecedented degree. And because of the satellite's orbital motion, new pairings will be generated and images produced at a much faster pace than is possible for systems that must depend on the Earth's rotation to alter dishes' relative positions. Furthermore, the space-based dish will be able to collect radio waves that have not suffered the distorting effects of the Earth's atmosphere, guaranteeing a new clarity of radio vision.

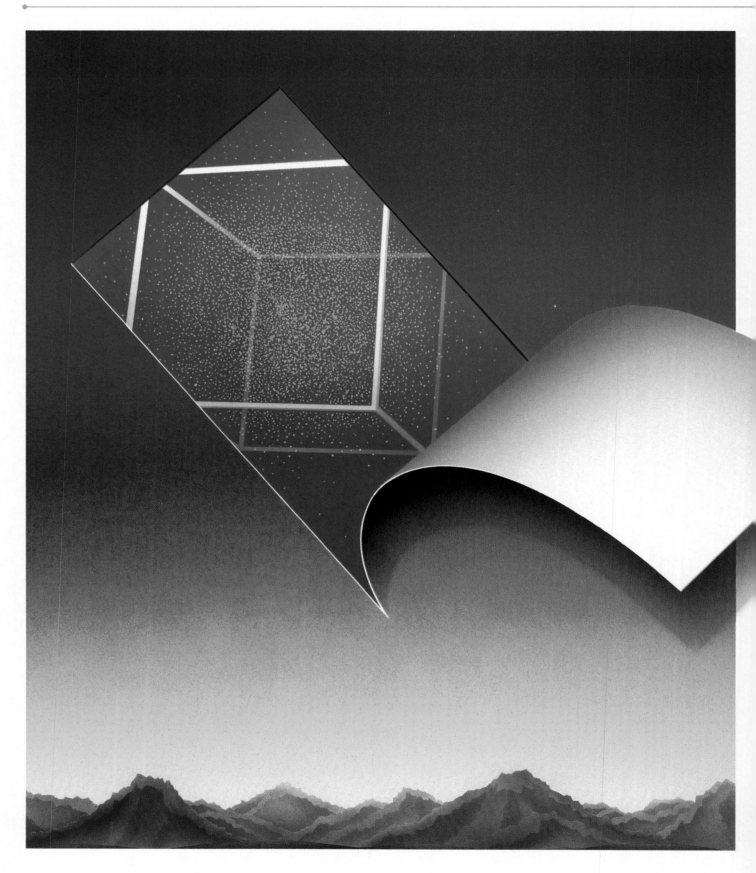

The Big
Picture

Like Dorothy, who dreamed that a tornado whisked her off to the Land of Oz, Adrian Melott lives in Kansas and takes imaginary trips through time and space. But there fact and fiction diverge, for Melott's travels are meticulously planned and have concrete scientific objectives. He is a cosmologist at the University of Kansas. Like dozens of other such researchers—astronomers and physicists by training—Melott pursues the age-old ideal of understanding the origin, evolution, and structure of the universe. In search of that elusive goal, he creates mathematical models of what the cosmos might have been like billions of years ago and then tests the models with the unparalleled calculating power of the computer.

Melott embarks upon his vicarious voyages into the universe of the past while seated at a terminal in his campus office in Lawrence. The terminal links him via telephone lines to a Cyber 205 supercomputer that is situated half a continent away at Princeton University's John von Neumann Computer Center. He has programmed the Cyber to represent a hypothetical cube of space at an early stage in the evolution of the universe—probably one million years after the birth of the cosmos. The cube contains many thousands of so-called particles, or markers—imaginary points of mass that represent clumps of matter weighing billions of times as much as the Sun. The velocity and position of each particle are dictated by equations derived from one theory or another of how the universe evolved.

When Melott types the command for the simulation to begin, his model universe streaks forward through time, covering billions of years in a matter of hours. Under the simulated tug of gravity, the force that binds together cosmic structures, the particles swirl around and eventually start to cluster. All the while, the computer is performing millions of operations per second in order to find out precisely how much gravitational attraction is exerted on each particle by all of the other particles. In this manner, the Cyber charts the changing velocity and position of each point of mass at intervals of a hundred million years or so. The simulation ends when it reaches the present.

Melott can have the voluminous numerical results converted by the computer into snapshots of the universe as it evolved in the model. Of greatest interest is the last picture of the series. Melott compares the swirls of particles in this computer-generated portrait of the universe with charts of the actual heavens prepared from photographs taken through telescopes. Melott is looking for a family resemblance, similarities in features like those that make brothers look like brothers, even to strangers. How closely the two images resemble each other in overall pattern and appearance tells the cosmologist whether the theory he tested is worth pursuing.

Computer modeling of the universe, of galaxies, and even of individual stars is transforming the way cosmologists do their work. Numerical models in themselves are nothing new. For centuries, astronomers have stated their theories in the form of complex mathematical equations that attempt to describe the things that telescopes reveal in the sky, explain how they got that way, and predict how they might evolve in the future. But unlike biologists and many other types of scientists, astronomers have lacked the means to actually experiment with their models.

The computer, by re-creating realms and events that happened only once, provides a laboratory where researchers can test their ideas and understanding. For today's astronomer, the possibility of staging such stupendous events as stellar collisions or the creation of galaxies is no longer out of reach. It is now simply a matter of getting access to sufficiently powerful computers and learning to write the appropriate software.

A SCIENCE RIPE FOR COMPUTERS

Astronomy's need for advanced calculating power was evident long before the advent of electronic computers. Because of the vast amount of computation involved in developing new ideas in this science, many years pass between the introduction of a theory and its confirmation through observation.

A classic example of this halting and arduous process is the saga that began with one of the founders of modern science, the seventeenth-century British mathematician and philosopher Isaac Newton. With a mental effort so immense that he later said it made his head ache, Newton worked out equations to explain the course of the Moon around Earth. His theory had to take into account not only the gravitational attraction exerted by the Sun, the Earth, and the other planets, but also the subtle variations in the Moon's orbit caused by slight irregularities in the spherical shapes of these bodies.

Simply gathering the data necessary to figure out whether Newton's theories of lunar motion were correct required two and a half centuries of observation and analysis. Finally, in 1919 at Yale University, Newton's transplanted countryman, Ernest Brown, published a three-volume table of mathematical functions describing every perturbation, however slight, in the elliptical path of the Moon around the Earth. But even this brilliant research—which was based on nearly a lifetime of Brown's own observations and analysis, and had the potential for laying to rest the last shreds of uncertainty about Newton's theories—could not be certified correct until it was spun out even further through massive computations.

The dramatic confirmation of Brown's work was made possible by technological developments in England. In the late 1920s, a crusty New Zealander named Leslie John Comrie had introduced punch-card tabulating machines to the government office responsible for publishing Britain's *Nautical Almanac,* a guide to navigation for seamen. Comrie later recalled that when Brown visited London in the summer of 1928 to witness the machines at work, the Yale astronomer experienced ''ecstasies of rapture'' at the speed of the calculations. Using these tabulators and Brown's tables, which contained nearly 100 million figures describing lunar motion, Comrie produced a volume predicting the precise position of the Moon at every noon and midnight from 1935 to the year 2000. Since the first day of January in 1935, there have been twice-daily proofs of Brown's calculations.

Brown's excitement over Comrie's primitive computing facility ignited the enthusiasm of a graduate student named Wallace Eckert, a soft-spoken young astronomer and mathematician. Eckert became obsessed by the mathematics of celestial mechanics, and in 1934, he established at Columbia University the first computing laboratory devoted to astronomical calculations. To equip his lab properly, he persuaded IBM to provide its best machines free of cost. The computing tools that IBM donated included not only up-to-date versions of the sorting and tabulating devices that were used by Comrie in England but also a punch-card multiplier that was tailored to Eckert's specifications. Eckert installed the equipment in the attic of Columbia's observatory, and in this humble home the new laboratory began undertaking computing chores for astronomers around the world.

AN HEIR TO WALLACE ECKERT'S LAB
Though Eckert left Columbia on the eve of World War II to oversee preparation of a nautical almanac for the U.S. Naval Observatory, the laboratory he had established at the university continued as a magnet for astronomers. One of them was a young astrophysicist named Martin Schwarzschild. The son of an astronomer, Schwarzschild was twenty-eight years old when he joined the Columbia faculty in 1940, shortly after Eckert's departure. Schwarzschild had a remarkable knack—"just good luck," he later called it—for being in the right place at the right time to take advantage of innovations in computers.

Early on, Schwarzschild had recognized the need for sophisticated computing tools. Even as a student at the University of Göttingen, he saw that the only way to prove or test a theory was to solve the equations that describe it—with real numbers derived from observational data. Often, the description takes the form of differential equations that predict the paths of moving objects in response to the tangible force of gravity. Solving differential equations by hand is onerous work, and Schwarzschild knew he would welcome any help he could get. Forced out of Germany by the Nazis in 1935, he accepted the first of several short-term posts: a year's fellowship at the University of Oslo studying pulsating stars.

Schwarzschild did his calculations in Norway with the help of an early analog computer, a copy of a machine called the differential analyzer built in 1930 by Vannevar Bush at the Massachusetts Institute of Technology. Schwarzschild's foresightful professor, Svein Rosseland, had commissioned the duplicate from a local instrument company.

The differential analyzer was a cumbersome device composed of "lots of mechanical parts, gears, and fast rotating disks turned by a crank," Schwarzschild recalls. But it was also the first machine capable of solving differential equations, and the young scientist put it to productive use as he developed a numerical model to explain the varying brightness and girth of pulsating stars. Because the differential analyzer performed its computations mechanically—by measuring movement and distance—it was much less accurate than the digital punch-card machines that Schwarzschild would encounter later. But it gave him good enough results that he was able to publish an influential paper on how stars can change in size and luminosity.

The year in Oslo led to a three-year fellowship at Harvard College Observatory, where Schwarzschild had the opportunity to make extensive firsthand observations of pulsating stars and gather an abundance of raw data on the subject before joining the Columbia University faculty in 1940. The computing facility at Columbia paid off immediately for Schwarzschild. He transferred his Harvard data to punch cards, and the numerical studies he produced from them enabled him to resolve the disparities between his theoretical models of pulsating stars and their actual behavior.

VON NEUMANN'S INFERNAL MACHINE

Schwarzschild served in the U.S. Army during World War II. Following his discharge in 1947, he left Columbia for a post at Princeton University. There he began perhaps the most intriguing phase of his odyssey on the frontier of computing. The age of the electronic computer had dawned, and its foremost theoretician, John von Neumann, was in residence at the nearby Institute for Advanced Studies (IAS). Von Neumann and a team of scientists and engineers were trying to build a faster, bigger, and better computer.

Schwarzschild knew von Neumann. They had met during the war at the army's Aberdeen Proving Ground in Maryland where von Neumann served as an influential civilian consultant to the Ballistic Research Laboratory. When they met again in Princeton, von Neumann was looking for challenging problems for the new IAS computer to solve during shakedown runs in 1950 and 1951. Von Neumann wanted complex problems that had been at least partially solved, so that he could check the computer's answers. By this time, Schwarzschild had advanced from his specialized analysis of pulsating stars to a more general consideration of the interior structure of stars. The formidable differential equations that his studies involved filled the bill nicely for von Neumann, who invited him to use the IAS computer.

The numerical models of stellar structure that Schwarzschild produced with the help of von Neumann's machine were rudimentary by today's standards—but so was the computer. Programs and data, loaded into the computer by means of perforated tape, first had to be coded in the machine's digital language of ones and zeros. Cathode-ray tubes—the same devices now used for computer monitors—had been cleverly adapted to serve as memory, which, though mammoth for its day, amounted to only five thousand bytes, or enough for about two and a half pages of typewritten text. Vacuum tubes, which constituted the computer's logic circuits, habitually overheated and blew out. "It was what we called professor-designed," says Schwarzschild, "built for its logic but terrible to maintain."

In spite of the difficulties, the young scientist came to depend heavily on von Neumann's machine and felt that it made an important contribution to his work. "The computer," Schwarzschild recalls, "was a tool with which to experiment and explore." He relied on it to cut through the drudgery of massive calculations, using the time saved to test additional solutions to his theoretical problems.

While astrophysicists like Schwarzschild used computers to test theories about the nature of individual stars, cosmologists were seeking to understand the structure of the entire cosmos: How the universe began; why it expands and whether it will someday begin to contract; how galaxies formed and why they seemed to arrange themselves in clusters. Von Neumann's computer and its immediate successors were so limited in speed and memory, however, that they offered little advantage over paper and pencil in the assault against computations that dwarfed Schwarzschild's requirements as the cosmos dwarfs a single star. Not until more powerful computers were introduced in the late 1960s did the machines become useful to cosmologists.

A BENEFICIARY OF EINSTEIN

The science of cosmology is not much older than the revolution in computers. It began, like so much of our understanding of the physical world, with the theories of Albert Einstein. In 1915, Einstein spelled out for the first time, in his General Theory of Relativity, the intimate relationship between matter, time, and space. Among other things, he proved that all measurements of time and distance depend on the motion of the observer, and that the matter contained in the universe profoundly influences its shape.

In the details of his equations, however, Einstein made a mistake—one which he later termed "the greatest blunder of my life." For all his radical genius, Einstein was wedded to the centuries-old view of the universe as an unchanging backdrop against which the stars and planets fulfill their lives. When his figures indicated that the universe was not in equilibrium, that it had to be either expanding or contracting, he refused to accept the evidence of his own logic. Instead, he tinkered with the equations. He invented a new factor—which he called the cosmological constant—to keep the universe stable.

Seven years later, in 1922, Einstein's equivocation was discovered by a young Russian scientist named Alexander Friedmann. A mathematician and meteorologist with a drooping moustache and a passion for hot-air ballooning (he once held the altitude record of 23,000 feet), Friedmann set the equations right. He dropped Einstein's cosmological constant and came up with a relativistic model of a universe that was con-

89

An Orbiting Observatory

Earth makes a poor observatory. Turbulence in the atmosphere distorts an earthbound view of the heavens like a flawed windowpane. And the air's content of dust and other impurities so effectively scatters and absorbs light that much of the universe cannot shine through.

Managing the observatory. Instructions for the Hubble telescope will originate at the Space Telescope Science Institute in Baltimore, Maryland, where requests for observation time will receive a thorough review. Upon approval, the experiments will be fitted by computer into a schedule that groups them to minimize observation time lost to aiming the telescope. Then the schedule will be forwarded to NASA's Goddard Space Flight Center near Washington, D.C. There, commands for the observatory will be formulated and, along with the schedule, dispatched by satellite to White Sands, New Mexico, the base station for the Tracking and Data Relay Satellite. Positioned in geosynchronous orbit, this communications link will always be in position to pass instructions to the observatory and to report telescope data by way of White Sands and Goddard to Baltimore.

But soon astronomy will literally rise above the problem. The remedy: an unmanned observatory called the Hubble Space Telescope, which will orbit above the planet's gaseous envelope at an average altitude of 370 miles. The Hubble telescope will peer as far as 14 billion light-years into the cosmos, deeper into space and farther backward into time than ever before. The volume of the optically observable universe will increase more than 300-fold. Stars forty times fainter than the dimmest ones visible from Earth will appear in numbers that will strain astronomers' abilities to catalog them. For cosmologists, the Hubble telescope offers the possibility of confirming hypotheses about the origin of the universe that have been tested only as computer models (pages 109-119).

The Hubble telescope could not exist without computers. They guided the precision grinding and polishing of the light-gathering primary mirror, half the size of Mount Palomar's 200-inch reflector. After the observatory is in orbit, they will control the communications system by which instructions are passed to the satellite and data is returned to Earth. And computers will be essential for operating the five principal instruments that will probe the cosmos for its secrets.

The Telescope at Work

In orbit, the Hubble Space Telescope is to be largely self-sufficient. With solar panels, the satellite will generate its own electricity to power computers and instruments. It has no steering thrusters to run out of fuel (gases expelled by thrusters would travel with the satellite and degrade the telescope's observations). Instead, changes in the observatory's orientation will be accomplished by fifty-five-pound motorized fly-wheels. Following the Newtonian principle that every action begets an equal and opposite reaction, the observatory will turn in response to computer-controlled rotation of the

Focusing on the stars. Light entering the telescope first strikes the primary mirror. A secondary mirror relays the reflection through a hole in the primary mirror and focuses an image at the fine-guidance sensors and other observatory instruments (*opposite*). The mirrors are supported by a rigid framework of graphite epoxy bars, a composite material that absorbs a small quantity of water during manufacture on Earth. The satellite's computer will make fine adjustments necessary to realign the mirrors as the framework shrinks from dehydration during the first weeks in orbit. Two solar panels provide electricity for the observatory through a bank of six rechargeable batteries.

Primary Mirror

Instruments

Solar Panel

Secondary Mirror

wheels. The telescope will always be oriented to keep bright sunlight from damaging the sensitive instruments inside. Should the satellite accidentally swing toward the sun, sensors will detect the increasing brightness and automatically close a protective door.

Rotated by the flywheels toward the object of an astronomical experiment, the satellite will use its fine-guidance system—an assembly of lenses and mirrors governed by a computer—to lock onto guide stars *(pages 99-101)* near the edge of the telescope image to keep the instrument pointed at the target. The center of the telescope's field of view will be reserved for an instrument called the wide-field planetary camera, which can be used for measuring distances between stars or can zero in for close-ups of objects in the Solar System. If the satellite is maneuvered appropriately, light from a target star or galaxy can also be directed to either of a pair of spectrographs that analyze the wavelengths, to a photometer for measuring brightness, or to the observatory's faint-object camera. This instrument is expected to reveal dim stars that have been obscured by the radiance of brighter neighbors.

Apportioning the view. Light passing through the hole in the primary mirror travels directly to some instruments and is reflected by so-called pick-off mirrors to others, shown separated in this drawing for clarity. A rectangular pick-off mirror deflects the center of the image toward the wide-field planetary camera. Three arc-shaped pick-off mirrors reflect the fringe of the image to the fine-guidance sensors. Other portions of the telescope's field of view pass through apertures to the observatory's other instruments: the two spectrographs, the photometer, and the faint-object camera.

Instruments

Fine-Guidance Sensor

Pick-Off Mirror

Apertures

Pick-Off Mirror

Wide Field Planetary Camera

93

tinuously expanding. In 1925, Friedmann died of typhoid at thirty-seven, and after his premature death, his revolutionary ideas were forgotten.

But in 1927, another researcher, the Belgian priest and astronomer Abbé Georges Lemaître, independently arrived at the same conclusions and published the results in an obscure scientific journal. Lemaître suggested that the cosmos began expanding from a dazzlingly brilliant fireball—the explosion of an enormous "primeval atom" of extremely hot and highly compressed matter. From this imaginative kernel of an explanation evolved the concept that is known today as the Big Bang theory of the universe.

THE CASE FOR EXPANSION

Lemaître's writings eventually came to the attention of the American astronomer Edwin Hubble, who was uniquely positioned to examine the notion of an expanding cosmos. In 1929, Hubble used Mount Wilson's powerful new 100-inch telescope to measure the spectra of light from recently discovered galaxies. When he compared these spectra to those of the Sun and of other stars close to the Earth, he was surprised to discover that the lines in the spectra were shifted toward the red end of the color scale. Upon further analysis, he realized that the shift was greatest in light from the most distant galaxies.

Hubble ascribed this red shift to the Doppler effect, which is a familiar phenomenon as it applies to sound but holds for light waves as well: As a source of noise—such as a car with a blaring horn—approaches a listener, the frequency of the sound waves increases, raising the pitch. As the car passes and moves away, frequency decreases and pitch becomes lower. In the same way, the waves of an approaching source of light have slightly increased frequency and the light looks bluer than it should. By showing that the opposite held true for the light from galaxies—that they looked a little too red—Hubble established that they were receding. Just as Friedmann and Lemaître had predicted, the cosmos was expanding.

Though the notion that the universe is ballooning outward soon became generally accepted, many cosmologists stopped short of accepting the Big Bang theory. During the late 1940s, a competing model came into vogue, asserting that the cosmos, though expanding, had no definable beginning. This so-called Steady State theory was set forth by three young astrophysicists at Cambridge University—Hermann Bondi, Thomas Gold, and Fred Hoyle. If true, however, the theory implied that galaxies should be farther apart than they are—unless, and as the astrophysicists proposed, matter was continuously and spontaneously created to fill the gaps left by expansion.

The ensuing debate between proponents of the two models, Big Bang and Steady State, raged throughout the 1950s and beyond, stimulating both the popular imagination and astrophysical research. Then in 1965, conclusive evidence turned up. Proponents of the Big Bang had theorized that some trace of what was once an intense field of microwave radiation should have survived as a relic of the primordial fireball and must now pervade the universe. The discovery of this cosmic radiation occurred at the Bell Laboratories, not far from the site where another Bell employee, Karl Jansky, had discovered the first radio signals from space. Researchers Robert Wilson and Arno Penzias were working on a huge microwave antenna, designed to relay telephone calls to communications satellites, when they encountered unexpected interference. The signal they discovered was of uniform intensity everywhere they searched in the sky. By locating this faint but ubiquitous primal echo, Penzias and Wilson had found proof that the cosmos must have had a fiery beginning.

NEW RIDDLES FOR COSMOLOGISTS

For theorists working on models of the structure of the universe, the new evidence of the Big Bang raised as many questions as it answered. The evenness of the radiation Penzias and Wilson found implied that elemental matter was uniformly distributed in the early universe. Yet from this apparent homogeneity had evolved the vast uneven clustering of galaxies that exists today.

When the universe was about 100,000 years old, theorists proposed, it was dense, hot, smooth, and virtually without structure. But during the first billion years or so, atoms of hydrogen had somehow clumped together to form clouds. Out of these clouds of hydrogen are thought to have condensed—in a sequence that is still not clear—the present-day hierarchy of heavenly bodies. Stars by the hundreds of billions gathered into galaxies. Galaxies came together by the hundreds or thousands in vast clusters. And the clusters clumped together into superclusters—ten or more clusters linked like beads on a string up to a billion light-years long.

To account for this clumpiness, cosmologists now assume that the early universe did not expand with the complete uniformity implied by the original Big Bang theory. Instead, they speculate, there were slight variations in the density of matter. That is, at some places, particles of matter were packed slightly closer together than at others. These minuscule irregularities were then compounded by the force of gravity; the more densely packed groups attracted other particles, thereby magnifying the gravitational effects. The growing aggregates of matter gradually evolved into the structures observable today.

EARLY COMPUTER MODELS OF THE COSMOS

The first researcher to attempt to model this process with a computer was James Peebles, a physicist and colleague of Martin Schwarzschild's at Princeton. A bespectacled man of scholarly demeanor, Peebles had been interested in mechanical things since his boyhood in Manitoba, Canada. He entered the University of Manitoba as an engineering student but switched to physics because, he explained later, he had "more friends in that department and the parties were better." When Peebles began computer modeling, he was thirty-four years old and already established as an influential figure in the field of cosmology. Among other accomplishments, he had been one of those responsible for predicting the nature of the background radiation detected by Penzias and Wilson.

Peebles was fascinated by the question of how galaxies came to form clusters in an expanding universe. In 1969, returning from a sabbatical leave spent at the California Institute of Technology, he stopped off for a month at Los Alamos National Laboratory in New Mexico. While there, he took advantage of the laboratory's powerful computer—a Control Data Corporation CDC 6600 that was ordinarily used in the design of nuclear weapons—to experiment with numerical simulations of cluster formation.

"The game," as Peebles puts it, "is to guess at initial conditions and move forward to the present." Using Fortran, the standard computer language for scientific projects, he wrote a program on punch cards to simulate the interaction of 300 independent chunks of matter under the influence of one another's gravity. Peebles called the chunks particles, and to each one he assigned a mass that approximated the amount of matter in a typical galaxy. To simplify his model universe, he made all the particles the same size. Before running the program, he fed into the computer the initial position of each particle, as well as its speed and direction of travel.

Peebles based the values for these factors on a combination of cosmological theory, intuition, and the arcane science of particle physics. He speculated that some of the ideas in this specialized branch of research, which investigates the constitution and interplay of subatomic entities, might well apply to the particles in his model, even though they were much larger and farther apart than the building blocks of atoms.

The model reenacted a process of cosmic evolution that probably took millions of years, but it was merely an overnight run on the computer. The CDC 6600 was programmed to record the numerical results of the simulation at selected intervals called timesteps, but there was also a camera set up to take pictures of a computer monitor, on which the arrangement of the particles was displayed at the end of each interval. The series of photographs showed a gradual change in the distribution of mass as the areas most densely populated with particles became even more crowded. This was precisely the result that Peebles had expected. In his words: "We wound up with what looked like a cluster of galaxies."

Returning to Princeton, Peebles continued to experiment with his new modeling technique, using the university's smaller and slower IBM 7094. He enlisted the help of a colleague, Edward Groth, who was a gifted programmer as well as a cosmologist. Groth made the simulations much more precise by developing more efficient algorithms for the programs. In spite of the improvements, the idea of computer modeling was so new and unorthodox that Peebles did not fully trust the results of his experiments and never published a major paper describing them. Instead, he and Groth made a short movie explaining their methodology and showing a simulation in which a cluster of galaxies formed. The film proved to be highly influential in persuading other cosmologists to create their own computer universes.

A BOTTOM-UP PICTURE OF CREATION

Peebles went on to demonstrate an undeniable statistical similarity between the distribution of particles in his model and of galaxies in the real universe. "What I saw in the galaxy statistics," he said later, "looked like a clustering hierarchy.

Clusters tend to appear in tight knots, which appear in knots of knots and so on." It seemed clear to Peebles that galaxies formed early and later came together as clusters. One of his heroes, the astronomer-priest Lemaître, had suggested as much nearly a half century earlier. In 1977, Peebles published a paper championing this small-to-large scenario, which became known as the "bottom-up" model of creation.

The bottom-up model accounted quite nicely for the formation of galaxies and clusters, but it faltered when called upon to rationalize the production of larger structures, such as superclusters. The problem was all in the timing. Theoretical calculations and increasingly sophisticated computer simulations by Peebles and others all seemed to show that the bottom-up process could not have produced superclusters quite soon enough. The evolution of such structures should have taken far longer than the 10 to 20 billion years that the universe has existed. There had to be a piece of the puzzle missing—or the bottom-up model was wrong.

A possible clue had come to light in one of Peebles's early computer models. He and a colleague, Jeremiah Ostriker, had sought to analyze the stability of disk galaxies—those that are shaped like pancakes. As in all galaxies, the particles representing groups of stars in the model were held in orbit by the force of gravity. The program called for the gravitational interaction of 300 particles distributed in a pattern typical of disk galaxies.

When Peebles and Ostriker ran the program, however, their simulated galaxy went haywire. "To our surprise, the disk went wildly unstable," said Ostriker. "The stars' orbits went from being nearly circular to being very eccentric." Some of the stars even became detached from the disk and flew off into space. Ostriker and Peebles decided that such chaos does not occur in a real galaxy because of some invisible reservoir of mass that possesses the additional gravity needed to prevent the disk from disappearing. Perhaps every galaxy, they suggested, is endowed with a huge amount of unseen mass. If so, cosmologists and their computer models were failing to take into account an important part of the cosmos.

THE PUZZLE OF HIDDEN MASS

The notion of invisible matter in the galaxies was not entirely new. The first hint that more is out there than meets the eye had come decades earlier in 1933, just four years after Edwin Hubble made his observations of the expanding universe. At that time, the brilliant Swiss-born astronomer Fritz Zwicky noted that individual galaxies in a distant group of galaxies known as the Coma cluster were moving much more rapidly than he had anticipated. Their speeds were so great that, according to the laws of celestial mechanics relating mass, velocity, and distance, the entire cluster should have been flying apart. Something besides the visible luminous matter had to be holding the cluster together, and Zwicky dubbed the hypothetical material "missing mass."

The question of missing or hidden mass has cosmic implications, for nothing less than the eventual fate of the universe may be at stake. The continued expansion of the cosmos depends upon the density of matter within it. If the average measure of mass per cubic meter is less than the so-called critical density, the universe will continue to expand forever. Scientists call this possibility an open universe. The prospect of hidden mass, however, raises the possibility that the universe is closed. If there is enough hidden mass, the combined gravitational forces of all the matter in the universe will eventually stop its expansion. Contraction will begin, and eventually the cosmos will collapse in a "Big Crunch."

Zwicky's astonishing assertion and the equally sensational results of Peebles and Ostriker's model were substantiated in the late 1970s by astronomer Vera Rubin and her colleagues at the Carnegie Institution in Washington, D.C. After several years of photographing the heavens through telescopes to measure the rotational velocities of more than seventy spiral galaxies, Rubin said: "The conclusion is inescapable. Mass, unlike luminosity, is not concentrated near the center of spiral galaxies. There has to be lots of mass farther out, beyond the visible disk."

The findings of Zwicky, Peebles, Ostriker, and Rubin all pointed to the same bizarre conclusion: Most of the mass in the universe is invisible. Cosmologists now estimate that nonluminous, hidden matter may constitute between 90 and 99 percent of all the mass in the universe. Unlike luminous matter, it neither emits light like stars nor absorbs it like the clouds of gas and dust that exist in many galaxies. By the end of the 1970s, the search for the identity of the dark matter had become a major preoccupation for cosmologists. And their primary investigative tool was the computer simulation.

NEUTRINOS UNDER SUSPICION

All manner of candidates have been suggested for the role of hidden matter. They range from cosmic dust and burned-out stars to hypothetical subatomic particles so exotic that they are immune to most physical forces and have never been observed on Earth.

One nominee was an elusive subatomic particle, the neutrino. These insubstantial bits of matter are released in torrents during nuclear reactions and are so plentiful that each thimbleful of space contains about a hundred of them. They are the smallest particles so far detected and can travel at nearly the speed of light. That neutrinos moved so rapidly and could not be contained by even the densest metals used as shielding against nuclear radiation suggested to physicists that neutrinos were something of a paradox—particles without mass. For a time, they were ignored in the search for dark matter.

Then in 1980, two independent teams of researchers—a U.S. group under Frederick Reines, codiscoverer of the neutrino, and a Soviet group headed by Victor Andreevich Lyubimov—reported that the particle appeared to have a trace of mass after all. As measured by the Soviets, it amounted to practically nothing—about one ten-thousandth the weight of an electron, at that time the lightest known particle. Even so, neutrinos are so numerous that cumulatively they could account for all of the missing mass.

To some researchers, moreover, the neutrino was a particularly appealing suspect because it fit nicely with their favorite theory of how the universe's biggest structures came into being. Their view, the brainchild of a brilliant Soviet theoretician named Yakov Zel'dovich, is known as the top-down scenario. In contrast to the bottom-up theory championed by James Peebles, which maintains that galaxies formed first and then coalesced into clusters

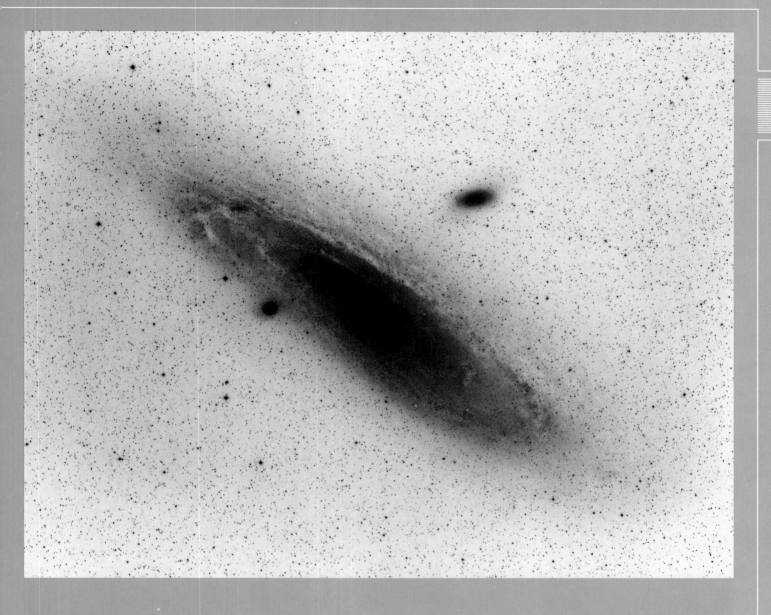

An Inventory of the Stars

Astronomers record the fruits of their observational labors in catalogs—lists of celestial objects that typically supply an identifying name (or number) for each object and include information about position, brightness, and other matters. Some of the catalogs created in the past have contained several hundred thousand entries.

But these compilations, representing decades of work by whole teams of astronomers, pale beside the Guide Star Catalog prepared for the Hubble Space Telescope *(pages 90-93).* In electronic form, it lists upward of 20 million stars whose magnitude—an astronomical measure of brightness—ranges from nine to fourteen. The Hubble telescope will use these beacons to fix a steady gaze on points in space.

As explained overleaf, computers have extracted the necessary stellar information for this catalog from conventional astronomical photographs like the one above, which shows the Andromeda galaxy. Called sky survey plates, these pictures are in the form of negatives (bright spots appear dark) and render the sky of both the Northern and Southern hemispheres in sharp detail.

From Sky Plate to Data Base

The Guide Star Catalog for the Hubble telescope was electronically derived from a total of 1,497 sky survey plates—high-quality astronomical photographs taken at Mount Palomar and at the Siding Spring Observatory in Australia over a period of several years. Each 200-square-inch plate was scanned by a device called a microdensitometer, which used a fine beam of light from a halogen lamp to discern details recorded in the emulsion. The scanning—a process that took twelve hours per plate—yielded brightness information in prodigious amounts: every square inch of the plates is broken into a million picture elements, or pixels. Computer programs analyzed this raw data to distinguish stars from other objects—such as galaxies—from empty space. The computer also selected stars that met the brightness requirements, took note of their locations, and entered them in the catalog. Altogether, the catalog contains more than 700 megabytes of data that, if printed, would cover thirteen boxes of computer paper.

When the Hubble Space Telescope goes into operation, ground-control computers will select guide stars for a target by first recalling its surroundings from the master data base and then placing the target within the area bounded by the arc-shaped fields of view, called pickles, of the satellite's fine-guidance sensors. Next, for the same area of space, computer software will extract guide stars from the Guide Star Catalog and select, from the stars that fall within the pickles, pairs to use for aiming the telescope.

To scan a sky survey plate, a beam of light about fifty microns wide—about the dimension of a needle's point—is reflected by a mirror through the plate. Dark spots, representing stars, galaxies, and other luminous objects, absorb part of the beam, which is then reflected toward a photomultiplier tube.

The photomultiplier tube converts the changing brightness of the light beam as it scans the plate into a varying electrical signal, amplifies it, and sends it to an analog-to-digital converter.

Analog-to-Digital Converter

Photomultiplier Tube

Mirror

Halogen Lamp

Mirror

Computers store the digital information arriving from the converter in a master data base *(below, left)*. At the same time they sort stars according to position and magnitude and enter them in the star catalog.

Computers

Guide Star Catalog

Master Data Base

This view of the Andromeda galaxy, displayed on a computer monitor, is reconstructed from a sky survey plate recalled from the master data base and combined with information from the Guide Star Catalog. Four guide stars appear as bright dots within the left-hand arc-shaped area on the screen, which represents the field of view of one of the Hubble telescope's three fine-guidance sensors. Guide stars in the other arcs are obscured by the brightness of the galaxy. Any of the guide stars are suitable for aiming the telescope at objects near the center of the instrument's field of view.

and superclusters, the top-down view portrays a universe in which the largest structures came first.

Top-town theorists believe that the predecessors of today's superclusters condensed from immense clouds of primordial gas. As the gas cooled and became denser, the clouds collapsed under the force of gravity into flattened shapes resembling pancakes millions of light-years in diameter. Many of these enormous structures survived and evolved into the superclusters visible today.

A neutrino with mass might provide a plausible mechanism for the top-down hypothesis. Though neutrinos travel at a velocity only slightly less than that of light, individual particles could nonetheless have been corralled by the colossal gravitational fields of the clouds envisioned by this theory. And having amassed in the primordial gas, neutrinos could have provided the mass that caused the clouds to change shape. Calculations suggested that an aggregation of neutrinos on such a grand scale—together with the ordinary matter inside the pancakes—would equal the estimated mass of a supercluster.

MODELING A NEUTRINO-DOMINATED UNIVERSE

All of these related developments—renewed interest in dark matter, evidence that neutrinos might represent the missing mass, and sharpening debate over top-down versus bottom-up scenarios—combined to generate a fever for computer simulations during the early 1980s. Perhaps because of the Soviet stake in the top-down scenario, scientists in the U.S.S.R. were the first to simulate the evolution of a neutrino-dominated universe. Researchers Fergei Shandarin and Anatoli Klypin produced enlightening models even though their computers lacked the speed and memory of machines then in use by Western scientists. An American cosmologist remembers attending a meeting in Italy in 1981 at which Shandarin could display the results of his simulations only by drawing pictures laboriously by hand.

Meanwhile, the computer modeler in Kansas, Adrian Melott, became infected with neutrino fever and began creating his own digital simulations of the early universe. Melott had been interested in computers even longer than he had been involved with cosmology. In 1963, while still attending high school in West Virginia, he had learned to program an IBM mainframe at a special summer institute for students gifted in mathematics. At the institute, he and a classmate attempted to produce a program that could set out a diet of 2,400 calories per day. The high-school students supplied the program with information about protein, vitamin, and calorie content of foods but neglected to tell the computer anything about the need for variety in a diet or about reasonable sizes for portions. When they ran the diet program, Melott recalls, one recommended menu consisted of "half of a chicken, a glass of skim milk, one egg, and twenty-seven heads of lettuce."

Young Melott was also a deeply religious person, and after receiving an undergraduate degree in physics from Bethany College, he went to divinity school and became a minister in the Unitarian-Universalist Church. By 1973, Melott had a pastorate in Tampa, Florida. One day, a member of his congregation—a professor at the University of South Florida—invited him to sit in on a course in general relativity.

The experience changed Melott's life. First, he earned a master's degree in physics. Then, in 1978, he left his pastorate to enroll full time in a doctoral program at the University of Texas. In the spring of 1980, Melott studied a semester at Oxford University, where he read a newspaper account describing how the Soviet team had measured the mass of the neutrino. The article launched him upon an academic career as a cosmologist.

Melott began his computerized investigation of the neutrino's role in the cosmos at Texas and continued the work at the University of Pittsburgh, where he did postdoctoral research in 1982 and 1983. He wrote programs in Fortran that modeled the top-down evolution of galaxies from a supercluster-size cloud of neutrinos, and his simulations gave intriguing preliminary results. For example, one model countered the doubts of some theorists that neutrinos could be slowed enough to settle in structures as small as galaxies. Melott demonstrated that the matter contained in a nascent galaxy exerted enough gravitational force to decelerate and capture about 10 percent of the neutrinos that attempted to pass through, a figure sufficient over millions of years to supply the mass needed to maintain the shapes of galaxies.

But Melott's early computer models were severely limited in the ways that they could simulate the universe. The biggest shortcoming was that they could only mimic the effects of gravity in one or two dimensions. To make the picture more complete, Melott began experimenting with three-dimensional simulations on a Digital Equipment Corporation DEC 20 minicomputer. He discovered, however, that he needed more computer speed and memory than the DEC 20 had to offer. Melott suspected that he needed a supercomputer—or at least a collaborator with access to one.

A CONVERT TO COMPUTER MODELING

During the summer of 1982 at a physics workshop in Aspen, Colorado, Melott found such a partner. She was Joan Centrella, a young physicist Melott had known during his years at the University of Texas. Unlike Melott, who had always felt comfortable with computers, Centrella had found the machines "intellectually odious" during her student days. She had taken a computer course as an undergraduate at the University of Massachusetts during the early 1970s and had worked with a cumbersome IBM mainframe that had to be programmed with punch cards. Centrella recalls "a campus computer center staffed by people who couldn't speak English to normal students. I was terribly turned off by it and gave up from frustration."

Centrella's aversion to computers even figured in her subsequent decision to pursue graduate studies at Cambridge University rather than in the United States. She suspected that the English university would put less emphasis on computers than would American graduate schools. This expectation proved only partially correct. For two years, she managed to work equations with pencil and paper as she labored over her thesis in cosmology. Then one day her faculty adviser called her into his office and announced: "Joan, it's time you learned to use the computer." He handed her a manual on Fortran.

With a little help from her friends—one of whom showed her how to log on to the university computer system in exchange for a Chinese dinner—Centrella learned very quickly. And as she acquired new computing skills, she began to discover the shortcomings of the computer hardware and software at Cambridge. Because the system had limited capabilities for displaying graphics, she had the results of one numerical experiment printed by a plotter. That process yielded a scroll that, when unfurled, stretched the entire length of the building where she was working.

At Cambridge, Centrella absorbed more than just the nuts and bolts of programming. She learned, for example, that "you can't get away with glossing over equations, making assumptions, and canceling terms. I felt that the work I did when I broke a problem down so I could solve it—bit by bit on the computer—reached a different level of understanding."

After earning her doctorate in England, Centrella spent a

year doing cosmological research and computer modeling at the University of Texas, where she crossed paths with Adrian Melott. Then, at the behest of Larry Smarr, a pioneer in computer simulations, Centrella joined the staff at the University of Illinois. By the time she and Melott renewed their acquaintance at Aspen in June of 1982, she more than shared his longing to use the most powerful computers for creating models of the cosmos. She had converted her wish into reality.

Centrella had secured an invitation to spend the summer at the Livermore National Laboratory in California. Livermore had what she and Melott wanted —a Cray-1 supercomputer. The Cray-1 was at that time the most powerful computer of all, capable of performing more mathematics in a second than a person could complete in a lifetime at a desk calculator. Centrella had been working on a one-dimensional model of a supercluster pancake that was very similar to Melott's work, so she and Melott agreed to collaborate in adapting the model to the Cray.

A LONG-DISTANCE TEAM

Distance hobbled the Melott-Centrella partnership from the beginning. During the summer of 1982, they worked nearly 3,000 miles apart—she at Livermore, he at Pittsburgh. Melott wrote segments of code for a new three-dimensional cosmic simulation on his DEC 20 computer. Lacking a computer communications link between the two sites, Melott mailed the finished components to Centrella on magnetic tape. She then linked the segments together and, enlisting help from colleagues at Livermore, adapted the resulting program to the supercomputer.

Centrella and Melott had to work quickly. They were eager to be the first team in the United States to simulate the evolution of a universe having a mass consisting predominately of neutrinos, and they knew that other researchers around the country were struggling toward the same goal. Moreover, Centrella had to leave Livermore for Illinois at the end of September. She soon found that the speed of the Cray—up to a hundred times faster than a minicomputer—enabled her to test their code and correct it much more rapidly than Melott could do the same job on his DEC 20. By the end of the summer, she recalls, ''Adrian and I were on the phone nonstop. We were actually debugging by phone. I would break off our conversation when the Cray became available, do a run, and if I found errors, call him up again. Oh, it was awful!''

The approach to simulations that Melott and Centrella developed while they were surmounting these problems became a prototype for other computer models of the cosmos. They knew that, even with a supercomputer, the universe they were creating had to have manageable dimensions. In their models, events beginning about 500,000 years after the Big Bang took place within an imaginary cube of space that represented a minuscule chunk of the expanding universe. Within this space, many thousands of particles moved in accordance with the dictates of gravity, although constraints in the program prevented collisions. Each particle represented a loose cloud composed of uncounted billions of neutrinos.

This technique for model building is known as the particle-mesh method because it sets up a three-dimensional grid—or mesh—defining thousands of cubes within the imaginary cube of space in order to simplify the calculation of gravitational forces working on each particle. There are several ways to operate within this framework.

The Melott-Centrella approach, which involved distributing the mass of each particle evenly throughout a space the size of one of the small cubes, is called the cloud-in-cell method *(pages 112-113)*. This technique permitted the two cosmologists to use up to a million particles—far more than the maximum of 2,000 used by James Peebles in the early 1970s—and attain a commensurate measure of realism. In a three-hour run on the Cray, the model calculated and recorded the speed, density, and position of each particle at nearly 200 timesteps as the model universe unfolded.

The Cray simulations produced impressive results. One version of the model grew enormous, neutrino-filled structures separated by yawning voids, a lacy pattern that resembled the clustering of galaxies in the real universe. Even more satisfying—and in marked contrast to the outcome of Peebles's models, which considered only luminous matter—the clusters required less time to form than the age of the universe. The popular press picked up the news of this patently evident success, Centrella recalls, and in the resulting euphoria, she and Melott "thought we had solved all the mysteries."

THE NEUTRINO TARNISHED

As the 1980s wore on, however, clues began to pile up that cast doubt on neutrinos as the missing mass. One tip-off, though inconclusive, was increasingly worrisome to many cosmologists: In the laboratory, no one had been able to confirm the initial measurements of the neutrino's mass. To make matters worse, in 1983, Marc Aronson of the University of Arizona reported an intriguing discovery about the dwarf galaxy Draco—a tiny neighbor of the Milky Way.

In an analysis reminiscent of the rotational studies performed by Vera Rubin in the 1970s, Aronson had measured the velocities of stars in Draco and found them to be moving so fast that he concluded, as Rubin had for larger galaxies, that Draco could only be held together by the gravity of its nonluminous matter. This was the first indication of hidden mass in a galaxy so small. It was also a strong indication that dark matter probably consists of something other than neutrinos. Those frisky particles move much too quickly to be trapped in a region with so little matter to attract them.

Then a new contender for the title of missing mass appeared. Its name is cold dark matter, or simply CDM. "Cold" refers to the low speed of this group of hypothetical subatomic particles believed to be left over from the early universe—photinos, gravitons, gravitinos, and others—compared to the high speed of the "hot" neutrino. The practice of predicting the existence of particles long before finding them is old hat to physicists. But these particles, proposed by physicists to balance equations that constitute various theories about the nature of matter, nonetheless recall Mark Twain's sardonic comment: "There is something fascinating about science. One gets such a wholesale return of conjecture out of such a trifling investment of fact."

But as possible components of cold dark matter—and as grist for computer simulations—these particles have great appeal to some cosmologists, especially advocates of James Peebles's bottom-up scenario for the formation of the cosmos. Predicted to be heavier and slower-moving than neutrinos, which may be too flighty to form anything smaller than superclusters, the particles of cold dark matter would presumably group together far more easily into small, galaxy-like clumps on the way to forming clusters and superclusters.

At the forefront in modeling a bottom-up universe in which cold dark matter predominates was an international trio of researchers. The alliance began in 1982 at the University of California at Berkeley with scholars from the United States, Great Britain, and Mexico. Marc Davis, the American, was a professor at Berkeley; he came to the group fresh from five years' observation work at Harvard, where he had helped chart locations and speeds for several thousand galaxies. Simon White, an Englishman, was also a member of the faculty at Berkeley and a veteran of computer modeling, having run simulations of cluster formation and galaxy collisions while a doctoral candidate at Cambridge University. Carlos S. Frenk, Mexican-born and British-educated, was a post-doctoral fellow in astronomy who had been an acquaintance of White's during his Cambridge days.

The Berkeley team had already experimented with models of a neutrino-dominated universe similar to those of Centrella and Melott, but they were not convinced by the results. "Neutrinos would not produce a universe that resembles what we see today," asserts Davis. When Davis, White, and Frenk decided to look elsewhere for the stuff of missing mass, they also had to search for a new approach to constructing numerical simulations. In their judgment, the techniques they had been using, though adequate for modeling the superclusters that begin the top-down evolution of the universe, were too coarse for simulating the formation of galaxies, the much smaller structures that appear early in the life of a bottom-up universe.

The Berkeley cosmologists happened upon a technique that would suit their purposes in the work of George Efstathiou, whom they recruited for their CDM project. An Englishman of Cypriot extraction on the faculty of Cambridge University's Institute of Astronomy, Efstathiou had developed his approach to modeling in collaboration with James Eastwood at the University of Durham during the late 1970s.

The method begins as a cloud-in-cell model. Those results are then refined by additional calculations that the Berkeley team estimated would yield gravitational attractions between particles five times as accurate as those obtained from the cloud-in-cell method alone. This plus was accompanied by a considerable minus—the computer time required for such precision limited the number of particles to 250,000 or so, about one-fourth the number used by modelers like Centrella and Melott. Fewer particles, like inaccurate assessment of gravity, would lead to inexact results, but the team was convinced that the net effect would be to simulate the evolution of the universe in sufficient detail to show the creation of the galaxy-size clumps of mass predicted for a universe governed by cold dark matter.

In the winter of 1983, the four researchers had a rare opportunity to work together for a stretch of several months, long enough to begin programming for a model based on cold dark matter. After that interlude in their regular duties, the collaboration became "a little chaotic," in the words of Simon White. Frenk returned to England and the University of Durham; White migrated to the University of Arizona. To keep in touch with one another, they consulted regularly by electronic mail, and each member of the group met periodically with one or more of the others to review their progress and divide up the workload.

If the number of particles in the model was limited to fewer than 33,000, the simulation could run to completion on VAX minicomputers—to which each of the collaborators had ready access—in about seventy hours. For Davis and company, three days' wait for results was a small inconvenience compared to the nuisance of borrowing time on a supercomputer. That independence ended in 1987. In order to increase the number of particles in their model to about 260,000, they arranged for time on a Cray X-MP at the National Science Foundation's Supercomputer Center in San Diego. Whether performed by a VAX or a Cray, the simulations required prodigious amounts of software. Before long, however, writing all the code had become second nature to the four men, who shared the duties. "Software development for an astronomer is almost like using a telescope," says Davis. "It has become a tool of the trade."

THE MYSTERY CONTINUES

To Davis and his colleagues, the results of the CDM models were encouraging. In the course of the simulations, particles formed agglomerations of mass reminiscent of galaxies, which then, true to the bottom-up scenario, came together in clusters that closely resembled the ones that astronomers see in the heavens. The model worked so well, Davis insists, that "there had to be some grain of truth to it."

Other interpreters—including James Peebles, who has adopted the view that cold dark matter may indeed be the missing mass—were considerably less sanguine. They noted that the CDM simulations, like the neutrino models that preceded them, start out well but fail to account for the later stages of cosmic evolution. In particular, CDM models have difficulty producing the lacy structure of superclusters and voids.

Yet the biggest problem for the theorists has nothing to do with the models themselves. No matter how likely or logical the concept of cold dark matter might seem to some cosmologists, it is nothing more than conjecture. Physicists have yet to detect a single photino, gravitino, or any of their cousins. The possibility remains that neither form of dark matter, cold or hot, comprises all of—or even any of—the hidden mass.

Whatever the case, the process of testing the possibilities by means of computer modeling has undeniably come of age. While the theorists seek new suspects in the secret of missing mass, researchers like Adrian Melott and Simon White are busily developing new and far more revealing simulations of cosmic evolution. Models of the future will move beyond the already complex analysis of gravitational interaction of particles to consider other variables, such as the behavior of gas in clouds and collisions between galaxies. These simulations will test the limits of even the most powerful computers, but the scientific payoff will be ever more realistic journeys through space and time.

Running the Cosmos by Computer

The computer models cosmologists build to test theories of the evolution and structure of the universe involve gargantuan amounts of data processing. The reason is this: The path through the cosmos of every galaxy, star, and speck of dust is affected by the gravitational field of every other galaxy, star, and speck of dust. Across the expanse of the universe, the attraction of one object for another may be subtle, but it is also cumulative. Over the 15 billion years that the universe is thought to have existed, even the weakest of gravitational forces has played a significant role in shaping the cosmos into the web of filaments, knots, and voids observable today.

To calculate all these effects is patently impossible, even for the fastest computers. Luckily, the mathematics of statistics permits cosmologists to sketch the evolution of the universe by analyzing a fraction of it—about a billionth of the total.

Excluding gases and dust, even this thimbleful of the cosmos might contain a hundred thousand galaxies, more than a computer could handle were it not for some computational shortcuts. One is to simplify the model, first by lumping together the mass within it and dividing the total equally among as few as 100,000 so-called particles, and then by calculating new positions for them at intervals—called time-steps—of 10 million years or so. Another is to use a mathematical ploy called the fast Fourier transform.

This variation of a technique invented by nineteenth-century mathematician Jean-Baptiste Fourier can calculate the pull of gravity exerted by all the particles on each other in about 1/10,000 the time (for a 100,000-particle model) that a computer would need to arrive at the result by considering each pair of particles individually.

However, for the Fourier operation to work its magic, matter within the model must be distributed so that it is concentrated at equal intervals, rather than spread about unevenly as it is in reality. A modeling technique called the cloud-in-cell method, explained on the following pages, reapportions matter without losing track of individual particles, a crucial feature. For the task of the model is to follow the course of each particle to see how closely the computer's results match those of the grandest experiment of all time.

Subdividing the Cosmos

A cosmological model of the universe takes place in a cube of space. Into this cube, the cosmologist instructs the computer to inject matter in the form of clumps called particles. Because cosmologists generally agree on the density of mass in the universe, the amount of matter in the model depends on the size of the cube being considered.

The number of particles, however, depends on the cosmologist's patience and budget for computer time: The more particles in the model, the more computer time necessary to process it. A typical model might contain between 100,000 and a million particles, each having the mass of a few billion suns. Running such a model may require at least ten hours' work by a Cray supercomputer.

To each particle, the model assigns a position, a speed, and a direction of travel. These assumptions about the dynamics of matter a few microseconds after the Big Bang are the essence of most hypotheses about the origin of the universe and are critical to the model's eventual outcome. If they are wrong, the model will grow into a form that bears little or no resemblance to the present-day universe.

At the outset, the computer holds the particles motionless while it calculates the change in direction and speed that each one would undergo in response to the combined gravitational tugs of all the other particles. To begin this process, the computer first subdivides the large cube into many smaller ones *(below)*.

Setting the stage. A blue cube, representing the starting point of a model of the universe, is superimposed here on a computer-generated image that shows a million galaxies linked in a lacy, filamentary structure. White spheres inside the cube symbolize equal-size clumps of mass calculated by dividing the total mass within the cube by the number of particles in the model. Some spheres are positioned closer than others to their neighbors in accordance with one of several theories about the distribution of matter within the universe an instant after it began.

Partitioning the cube. As a first step toward creating the regular spacing required by the fast Fourier transform, the computer subdivides the cube of space that is to be modeled into smaller cubes called cells *(right)*. Each corner of a cell is called a grid point. This grid of sixty-four cells is a simplified version of an actual model, which typically contains 262,144 cells.

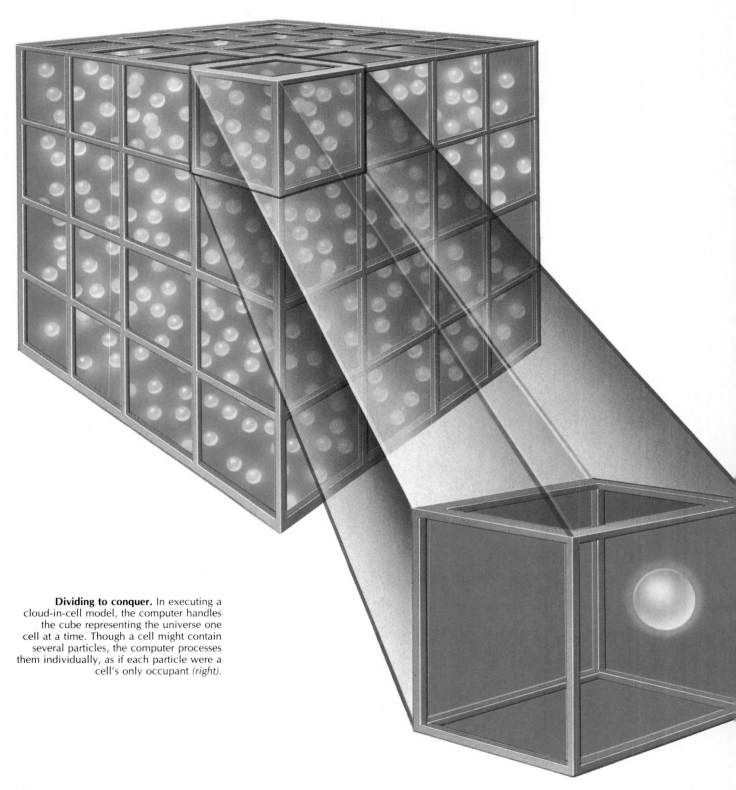

Dividing to conquer. In executing a cloud-in-cell model, the computer handles the cube representing the universe one cell at a time. Though a cell might contain several particles, the computer processes them individually, as if each particle were a cell's only occupant *(right)*.

The Cloud-in-Cell Method

For the fast Fourier transform to calculate the gravitational effect of all of a model's particles on each of the others, the mass of the particles must be transferred from within the cells of the model universe to the grid points.

One method of accomplishing this, used by early modelers, was simply to assign a particle's total mass to the nearest grid point, a crude technique that had significant shortcomings. For example, as a model evolved, the influence of one particle on another was often suddenly altered or even reversed as the first particle advanced across a cell and abruptly became assigned to a different grid point. Such mercurial changes do not occur in the real universe, and they made the models unacceptable.

These effects are greatly reduced with a technique called the cloud-in-cell method. In this approach, the computer handles the mass of each particle not as if it occupied a point but as if it were spread uniformly throughout a space having the same volume as a cell (below). This cloud of mass is then apportioned among each of a cell's eight grid points, as shown overleaf.

Like any simulation, a cloud-in-cell model of the universe is an approximation of reality. For example, most models do not take into account the mass of the gases that permeate the universe, nor do they allow for particle collisions, which could represent the effects of galaxies in the real universe smashing through each other. Cosmologists are willing to exchange such details, which would hardly alter the outcome of the experiment, for speed in processing the model.

From particle to cloud. The computer considers each particle of matter as a cell-shaped cloud (purple), centered on the particle and having the particle's mass distributed evenly throughout its volume. Depending on a particle's position within a cell, the cloud may extend into adjacent cells.

Converting Mass into Gravity

The final steps of the cloud-in-cell technique transfer the mass of a particle to nearby grid points *(below)*. As a result, individual particles disappear for a time, though the computer remembers their positions within the cells for later use.

In dividing each particle's mass among neighboring grid points, the computer positions all the model's matter at regular intervals throughout the grid, ready for the fast Fourier transform and other mathematical operations that convert the mass accumulated at grid points into gravitational fields.

Just as gravitational fields in the real universe hold the Earth in orbit around the Sun, gravity that builds at the model's grid points influences the paths of the particles of matter used in the simulation, as shown on the next pages. And even though the mass at each grid point is taken only from particles in the eight cells that share it, the nature of the fast Fourier transform assures that the contribution of every particle in the model, no matter how distant, is incorporated into the gravitational fields calculated for each grid point.

Apportioning mass. After creating clouds for the particles, the computer divides the cells of the model universe into eight equal sections, one for each of a cell's grid points *(below)*. The computer then calculates the fractions of each cloud that fall within the cell sections that it occupies, including sections of adjacent cells. Then an identical fraction of the particle's mass is assigned to the corresponding grid point *(below, right)*. As the process continues, white balls grow at grid points in proportion to the mass assigned there.

Transforming for force. When all the mass in the model universe has been assigned to grid points, the cube undergoes a series of mathematical operations, including a fast Fourier transform. The effect is to convert the mass into gravitational fields *(glowing balls)*.

Preparing to move. After initial processing by the computer, the model has a gravitational field not only at grid points along the outside of the cube, but at every one within the model as well. Next, the computer will reintroduce the particles to the model in preparation for moving them to new positions based on the influence of the gravitational fields *(right)*.

Completing a Timestep

Applying the fast Fourier transform to the model consumes about one-half the work required to advance the entire grid through one timestep in its evolutionary progress. The remainder is devoted to calculating the effects of the gravitational fields on individual particles. For a model that contains 500,000 particles, this operation requires in excess of 12 million calculations.

To make these calculations, the computer again handles particles one at a time, recalling from memory the fraction of each particle's mass that had been apportioned earlier to each of the eight nearby grid points *(page 114)*. Applying this factor to the gravitational fields created by the fast Fourier transform, the computer reckons the accelerating force exerted on each particle.

This process requires twenty-four calculations for each particle, or three per grid point. One of the calculations fixes the vertical force on a particle, the second figures the force exerted horizontally along the model's east-west axis, and the third calculates the force along the north-south axis. Added together, these components result in a single force that tugs on the particle. Applying this force for the duration of the model's timestep, the computer determines the particle's new position, which becomes the starting point for calculating the outcome of the next timestep *(page 113)*.

Moving masses. Recalling the original positions, speeds, and directions of travel of the model's particles, the computer calculates the effects, on each particle, of the gravitational fields at the corners of the cell that it occupies *(above, left)*. Applying the results to each particle over the duration of the model's timestep, the computer calculates a new position for each particle and moves it there, at the same time updating its speed and direction of travel *(above, right)*.

Watching the Universe Evolve

A typical cosmological model takes a few minutes on a Cray computer to advance one timestep, depending on the number of particles in the model. The length of a timestep varies as the model progresses. At the beginning, when matter launched outward by the Big Bang is moving at high speed, the timestep may be as short as one million years. Toward the end of the model, after particles have slowed, the timestep may be increased to a few hundred million years. By the time a model has run its course, the distribution of matter in the universe will have been determined for each of the model's hundreds of timesteps, several of which are represented by the blue cubes on these pages. As the model advances, two things happen: The universe expands; and the particles arrange themselves into patterns that look like the clusters of matter in the real universe.

To ascertain how closely the results of the experiment resemble the universe of today, the model's last timestep is analyzed statistically. One such test, called the correlation function, instructs the computer to measure the distances between each particle and all the others in the model. For a 500,000-particle model, 125 billion measurements are necessary. The distances are then used to calculate the probability that a particle will be found within a given distance of another. The outcome is compared to the result of the same calculation made from measurements of the distances between comparable clumps of matter—galaxies—in the real universe. The closer the probabilities, the more successful the model.

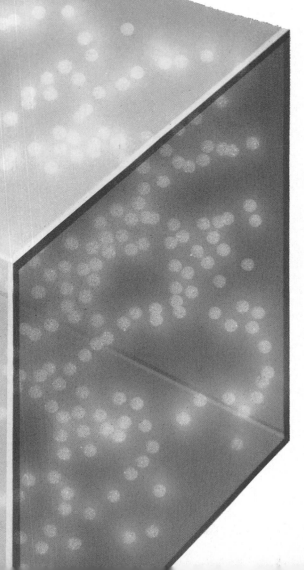

119

Glossary

Absolute zero: a temperature of zero degrees Kelvin (minus 273 degrees Celsius); the lowest possible temperature.

Algorithm: a step-by-step procedure for solving a problem.

Analog-to-digital converter: a device that changes an analog signal into digital form.

Aperture: the diameter of the lens or mirror in a telescope, which determines the instrument's capacity for gathering light or other forms of electromagnetic radiation; any opening or open space.

Aperture synthesis: in radio astronomy, using Earth's rotation to artificially create the advantages of a very large radio antenna.

Arc minute: an angle equal to one-sixtieth of a degree.

Arc second: an angle equal to one-sixtieth of an arc minute, or 1/3,600 degree.

Astrometry: a branch of astronomy concerned with precisely determining the positions of celestial objects.

Astronomy: the study of celestial objects.

Astrophysics: the study of the composition of astronomical objects and the physical laws that govern them.

Atom: the smallest unit of an element that possesses the chemical properties of the element.

Big Bang: according to a widely accepted theory, the primeval moment, 15 to 20 billion years ago, when the universe began expanding from a single point.

Binary stars: a pair of stars formed at the same time and orbiting around a mutual center of gravity.

Bit: the smallest unit of information in a computer, equivalent to a single zero or one. The word *bit* is a contraction of "binary digit."

Black hole: theoretically, an extremely compact body with such great gravitational force that no radiation can escape from it.

Blue shift: a Doppler effect seen when a light source is approaching an observer.

Brightness: the amount of light received from an object, which is the combined result of its actual luminosity, its distance, and any light absorption by interstellar dust or gas.

Byte: a sequence of bits, usually eight, treated as a unit for computation or storage.

Catalog: a published list of astronomical objects and their precise positions.

Cathode-ray tube (CRT): a television-like display device with a screen that lights up where it is struck from the inside by a beam of electrons.

Celestial coordinates: a pair of numbers designating an object's location on the celestial sphere. One coordinate, declination, is a north-south value similar to latitude; the other, right ascension, is similar to longitude.

Celestial mechanics: the study of the motions and gravitational interactions of celestial objects.

Celestial sphere: the apparent sphere of sky that surrounds the Earth; used by astronomers as a convention for specifying the location of a celestial object.

Central processing unit (CPU): the part of a computer that interprets and executes instructions. It is composed of an arithmetic-logic unit, a control unit, and a small amount of memory.

Charge-coupled device (CCD): an array of electromagnetic-radiation detectors, usually positioned at a telescope's focus.

Cloud-in-cell method: a computer modeling technique used to simulate the gravitational interaction of many points of mass in space.

Color enhancement: the technique of extracting as much information as possible from digital images by exaggerating small differences in color.

Cosmology: the study of the universe as a whole, including its large-scale structure and movements, its origin, and its ultimate fate.

Data base: a collection of facts about a particular subject or related subjects, divided into individual files and records that are organized for easy access.

Density: mass per unit of volume.

Digital: pertaining to the representation or transmission of data through numerical values.

Doppler effect: a wave phenomenon in which wavelengths appear to shorten as their source approaches the observer, or lengthen as the source recedes from the observer.

Electromagnetic radiation: radiation consisting of periodically varying electric and magnetic fields that vibrate perpendicularly to each other and travel through space at the speed of light.

Electron: a negatively charged particle that orbits the nucleus of an atom.

False coloring: a method by which colors are assigned to digital intensity values in astronomical imaging.

Fast Fourier transform: a computational technique used to speed the resolution of complex phenomena into their simpler components, and vice versa; makes possible computer models of the universe and the production of images from radio waves.

Field of view: the area of sky that is seen by a telescope.

Focal point: where the electromagnetic waves gathered by a lens or mirror are brought together (focused) to form an image.

Fortran: a computer language used primarily for scientific purposes.

Frequency: the number of times per second that a wave cycle (one peak and one trough) repeat.

Galaxy: a system of stars, gas, and dust that contains from millions to hundreds of billions of stars.

Gamma rays: the most energetic form of electromagnetic radiation, with the highest frequency and shortest wavelength. Because the Earth's atmosphere absorbs most radiation at this end of the spectrum, gamma-ray astronomy must be performed in space.

Gravity: the mutual attraction of separate masses; a fundamental force of nature.

Guide star: a star tracked by a telescope during an observation to ensure that the instrument remains trained on a specific target.

Hardware: the physical apparatus of a computer system.

Hydrogen: the most common detectable element in the universe, consisting of a single proton and electron in its usual form.

Infrared: a band of electromagnetic radiation having a lower frequency and a longer wavelength than visible light; most infrared radiation is absorbed by the Earth's atmosphere, but certain wavelengths can be detected from Earth.

Interferometry: a process in which a source of electromagnetic radiation is viewed simultaneously from two or more points for the purpose of improving resolution.

Jet: a thin, high-speed stream of charged particles ejected from the center of a radio source.

Language: a set of rules or conventions to describe a process to a computer.

Light: electromagnetic radiation visible to the naked eye.

Light-year: an astronomical unit of measurement equal to the distance light travels in a vacuum in one year; approximately six trillion miles.

Magnetic tape: plastic tape coated with a magnetic material on which information can be stored.

Magnitude: a designation of the brightness or luminosity of a celestial object.

Mainframe computer: the largest type of computer, usually capable of serving many users simultaneously.

Mass: a measure of the total amount of material in an object, determined either by its gravity or by the force necessary to change its velocity.

Microcomputer: a computer based on a microprocessor and intended to be used by an individual; often referred to as a personal computer.

Microprocessor: a single chip, containing all the elements of a computer's central processing unit; sometimes called a computer on a chip.

Model: a computer program that simulates complex physical phenomena through the manipulation of mathematical equations.

Molecule: the smallest unit of a chemical compound that can exist independently. Molecules are usually made up of many atoms bound together.

Neutrino: a subatomic particle, having little or no mass, that travels at nearly the speed of light.

Output: the data presented by a computer either directly to the user, to another computer, or to some form of storage.

Parallel: refers to a computer's handling of data or instructions in groups of several bits at a time rather than one bit at a time.

Photometer: an instrument used to measure light intensity.

Photon: a unit of electromagnetic energy associated with a specific wavelength.

Pyrex®: glass that contains an oxide of boron, making it resistant to heat.

Quasar: a quasi-stellar object; believed to be a galaxy at an early stage of development and emitting radiation of great intensity from its central region.

Radio waves: the least energetic form of electromagnetic radiation, with the lowest frequency and longest wavelength.

Real time: pertains to computation that is synchronized with a physical process.

Red shift: a Doppler effect seen when a light source is receding from the observer.

Refraction: the bending of light or other electromagnetic waves as they cross the boundary between media of differing densities—space and the Earth's atmosphere, for example.

Resolution: the degree to which details in an image can be separated, or resolved; the resolving power of a telescope is usually proportional to the diameter of its mirror.

Sensor: a device that converts physical energy such as heat or light into an electrical signal, which may then be translated for use by a computer.

Software: instructions, or programs, designed to be carried out by a computer.

Spectrograph: any device or instrument used to measure the wavelength of light from an object.

Spectrum: the array of colors, or wave frequencies, obtained by dispersing light, as through a prism.

Star: a gaseous, self-luminous object creating energy through nuclear reactions at its core.

Supercomputer: a term applied to the fastest, most powerful computers at a given time; supercomputers typically are used to solve scientific problems that involve the creation of mathematical models and the manipulation of large amounts of data.

Supernova: an explosion of a star that expels all or most of the star's mass and is extremely luminous.

Telescope: an instrument used to form images of distant objects. Telescopes are either reflective, using curved surfaces to reflect electromagnetic radiation to a focal point, or refractive, using lenses to focus radiation by bending it.

Twenty-one-centimeter line: a spectral line produced by hydrogen at a radio wavelength of just over twenty-one centimeters.

Ultraviolet: a band of electromagnetic radiation with a higher frequency and shorter wavelength than visible light. Most ultraviolet is absorbed by the Earth's atmosphere, so ultraviolet astronomy is normally performed in space.

Variable star: a star that changes in luminosity over time. Some variable stars change predictably and repeatedly, others unpredictably or only once.

Velocity: the rate that a distance is traveled per unit of time.

Wavelength: the distance from crest to crest or trough to trough of an electromagnetic wave; related to frequency—the longer the wavelength, the lower the frequency.

X rays: a band of electromagnetic radiation that has a wavelength between ultraviolet and gamma rays. Because X rays are completely absorbed by the atmosphere, X-ray astronomy must be performed in space.

Bibliography

Books

Bartusiak, Marcia, *Thursday's Universe*. New York: Times Books, 1986.

Berman, Louis, and J. C. Evans, *Exploring the Cosmos*. Boston: Little, Brown and Company, 1983.

Christiansen, W. N., and J. A. Högbom, *Radiotelescopes*. Cambridge: Cambridge University Press, 1985.

Clark, David H., *The Cosmos from Space*. New York: Crown Publishers, 1987.

Ferris, Timothy, *Galaxies*. New York: Stewart, Tabori & Chang, 1982.

Giacconi, Riccardo, and Herbert Gursky, *X-Ray Astronomy*. Dordrecht, Holland: D. Reidel Publishing Company, 1974.

Hall, Douglas S., Russell M. Genet, and Betty L. Thurston, eds., *Automatic Photoelectric Telescopes*. Mesa, Ariz.: The Fairborn Press, 1986.

Harwit, Martin, *Cosmic Discovery*. New York: Basic Books, 1981.

Henbest, Nigel, and Michael Marten, *The New Astronomy*. Cambridge: Cambridge University Press, 1983.

Hey, J. S., *The Radio Universe*. New York: Pergamon Press, 1983.

Kaufmann, William J., *Universe*. New York: W. H. Freeman and Company, 1987.

Learner, Richard, *Astronomy through the Telescope*. New York: Van Nostrand Reinhold Company, 1981.

Mitton, Simon, ed., *The Cambridge Encyclopaedia of Astronomy*. London: Trewin Copplestone Publishing, 1977.

Moore, Patrick, ed., *The International Encyclopedia of Astronomy*. New York: Orion Books, 1987. .

Moreau, R., *The Computer Comes of Age*. Cambridge: The MIT Press, 1984.

Sagan, Carl, *Cosmos*. New York: Random House, 1980.

Shipman, Harry L., *Black Holes, Quasars, and the Universe*. Boston: Houghton Mifflin Company, 1980.

Thompson, A. Richard, James M. Moran, and George W. Swenson, Jr., *Interferometry and Synthesis in Radio Astronomy*. New York: John Wiley & Sons, 1986.

Trefil, James S., *Space Time Infinity*. New York: Pantheon, 1985.

Tucker, Wallace, and Riccardo Giacconi, *The X-Ray Universe*. Cambridge: Harvard University Press, 1985.

Tucker, Wallace, and Karen Tucker, *The Cosmic Inquirers*. Cambridge: Harvard University Press, 1986.

Verschuur, Gerrit L., *The Invisible Universe Revealed*. New York: Springer-Verlag, 1987.

Periodicals

Angier, Natalie, "Better Spyglass on the Stars." *Time*, January 21, 1985.

Bahcall, John N., and Lyman Spitzer, Jr., "The Space Telescope." *Scientific American*, July 1982.

Boss, Alan P., "Collapse and Formation of Stars." *Scientific American*, January 1985.

Boyd, Louis J., Russell M. Genet, and Douglas S. Hall, "APT's: Automatic Photoelectric Telescopes." *Sky and Telescope*, July 1985.

"Caltech to Build 10-Meter Telescope." *Astronomy*, April 1985.

Cornell, James, "On a Mountaintop in Arizona, Things Are Starting to Look Up." *Smithsonian*, May 1979.

"Cosmic Modeling: How to Pack the Universe into a Cray." *Cray Channels*, Vol. 6, No. 4, 1984.

DiCicco, Dennis, "The Journey of the 200-Inch Mirror." *Sky and Telescope*, April 1986.

Efstathiou, George, et al., "Numerical Techniques for Large Cosmological N-Body Simulations." *The Astrophysical Journal Supplement Series*, February 1985.

Frenk, Carlos S., et al., "Cold Dark Matter: The Structure of Galactic Haloes and the Origin of the Hubble Sequence." *Nature*, October 17, 1985.

Genet, Russell M., et al., "The Automatic Photoelectric Telescope Service." *Publications of the Astronomical Society of the Pacific*, July 1987.

Giacconi, Riccardo, "The Einstein X-Ray Observatory." *Scientific American*, February 1980.

Hut, Piet, and Gerald Jay Sussman, "Advanced Computing for Science." *Scientific American*, October 1987.

Janesick, James, and Morley Blouke, "Sky on a Chip: The Fabulous CCD." *Sky and Telescope*, September 1987.

Kellermann, Kenneth I., and A. Richard Thompson:
"The Very Long Baseline Array." *Science*, July 12, 1985.
"The Very-Long-Baseline Array." *Scientific American*, January 1988.

Kristian, Jerome, and Morley Blouke, "Charge-Coupled Devices in Astronomy." *Scientific American*, October 1982.

Labeyrie, Antoine, "Stellar Interferometry: A Widening Frontier." *Sky and Telescope*, April 1982.

Learner, Richard, "The Legacy of the 200-Inch." *Sky and Telescope*, April 1986.

Levy, G. S., et al., "Very Long Baseline Interferometric Observations Made with an Orbiting Radio Telescope." *Science*, October 1986.

McAlister, Harold A., "Binary-Star Speckle Interferometry." *Sky and Telescope*, May 1977.

Mallove, Eugene F., "The Cosmos and the Computer: Simulating the Universe." *Computers in Science*, September/October 1987.

Maran, Stephen P., "A New Generation of Giant Eyes Gets Ready to Probe the Universe." *Smithsonian*, June 1987.

"Massive Clusters of Galaxies Defy Concepts of the Universe." *New York Times*, October 10, 1987.

Melott, Adrian L.:
"Cosmology on a Computer." *Astronomy*, June, July 1983.

"The Invisible Universe." *Astronomy,* May 1981.

Napier, Peter J., A. Richard Thompson, and Ronald D. Ekers, "The Very Large Array: Design and Performance of a Modern Synthesis Radio Telescope." *Proceedings of the IEEE,* November 1983.

Overbye, Dennis:

"The Great Telescope Race." *Discover,* May 1981.

"The Shadow Universe." *Discover,* May 1985.

Peebles, P. J. E.:

"The Mean Mass Density of the Universe." *Nature,* May 1, 1986.

"The Origin of Galaxies and Clusters of Galaxies." *Science,* June 1984.

Readhead, Anthony C. S., "Radio Astronomy by Very-Long-Baseline Interferometry." *Scientific American,* June 1982.

Sackett, Penny D., "A Computer-Generated Cosmic Portfolio." *Science News,* October 29, 1983.

Sellwood, J. A., "The Art of N-Body Building." *Annual Review of Astronomy and Astrophysics,* 1987.

Silk, Joseph, Alexander S. Szalay, and Yakov B. Zel'dovich, "The Large-Scale Structure of the Universe," *Scientific American,* October 1983.

Thomsen, Dietrick E., "Big Telescopes on a Roll." *Science News,* September 12, 1987.

Tyson, J. Anthony, "Low-Light-Level Charge-Coupled Device Imaging in Astronomy." *Journal of the Optical Society of America A,* December 1986.

Waldrop, M. Mitchell, "The Mirror Maker." *Discover,* December 1987.

Wells, Donald C., "Interactive Image Analysis for Astronomers." *Computer,* August 1977.

Wilford, John Noble, "Massive Clusters of Galaxies Defy Concepts of the Universe." *New York Times,* November 10, 1987.

Other Publications

Array Telescope Computing Plan: Proposal to the National Science Foundation. Charlottesville, Va.: National Radio Astronomy Observatory, September 1987.

Astronomy and Astrophysics for the 1980's, Vol. 1, *Report of the Astronomy Survey Committee,* and Vol. 2, *Reports of the Panels.* Washington, D.C.: National Academy Press, 1983.

Brocious, Daniel, "Automatic Photoelectric Telescopes Focus on Nighttime Sky." *Research Reports,* Spring 1987.

Burke, Bernard F., "Orbiting VLBI: A Survey." *VLBI and Compact Radio Sources.* Symposium No. 110, International Astronomical Union. Dordrecht, Holland: D. Reidel Publishing Company, 1984.

California Association for Research in Astronomy. Segments 1-7, August 1987.

Carlberg, Raymond, "Gas and Dark Matter in Cosmological 'Experiments.' " *Projects in Scientific Computing,* Pittsburgh Supercomputing Center, 1986/1987.

Cawson, M. G. M., J. T. McGraw, and M. J. Keane, "The CCD/Transit Instrument (CTI) Data-Analysis System." Preprints of the Steward Observatory, No. 691. Tucson: University of Arizona.

Centrella, Joan M., and Adrian L. Melott, "The Large-Scale Structure of the Universe: Three-Dimensional Numerical Models." *Numerical Astrophysics,* 1985.

Challenges to Astronomy and Astrophysics: Working Documents of the Astronomy Survey Committee. Washington, D.C.: National Academy Press, 1983.

"Current Developments at the MMT, 1986," Technical Report No. 20. University of Arizona and the Smithsonian Institution, June 1987.

"Engineering Reports on the MMT OSS, Tracking, Co-Alignment and Co-Phasing," Technical Report No. 21. University of Arizona and the Smithsonian Institution, June 1987.

Goring, W. P., D. K. Gilmore, D. B. McClain, and J. W. Montgomery, "MMT Computer Systems." *Proceedings of SPIE-The International Society for Optical Engineering.* Tucson, Ariz.: The Society of Photo-Optical Instrumentation Engineers, 1982.

Light Paths. Amado, Ariz.: Fred Lawrence Whipple Observatory.

McGraw, J. T., M. G. M. Cawson, and M. J. Keane, "Operation of the CCD/Transit Instrument (CTI)." Preprints of the Steward Observatory, No. 693. Tucson: University of Arizona.

"MMTO Visiting Astronomer Information." University of Arizona and the Smithsonian Institution, October 1987.

National Academy of Sciences, Astronomy Survey Committee: *Astronomy and Astrophysics for the 1970's,* Vol. 1, *Report of the Astronomy Survey Committee,* and Vol. 2, *Reports of the Panels,* 1973.

"New Generation Telescopes: The MMT Comes of Age." *Report on Research,* Tucson: University of Arizona, Spring/Summer 1987.

Operating the Hubble Space Telescope. NASA Publication.

Sellwood, J. A., "The Art of N-Body Building." *Annual Review of Astronomy and Astrophysics,* 1987.

Space Telescope. NASA Publication EP-166.

"Telescopes as Big as the Earth." In *Frontiers of Science,* Reports from the National Science Foundation. Washington, D.C.: Government Printing Office, 1977.

Vanden Bout, Paul A., *The Impact of the Information Age on Radio Astronomy.* Charlottesville, Va.: National Radio Astronomy Observatory, 1985.

Weekes, Trevor C., ed., "The MMT and the Future of Ground-Based Astronomy," Cambridge, Mass.: Smithsonian Astrophysical Observatory, 1979.

Picture Credits

Credits for illustrations in this book are listed below. Credits from left to right are separated by semicolons, from top to bottom by dashes.

Cover: Art by Stephen R. Wagner. 6: John R. Dickel, Stephen S. Murray, Jeffrey Morris, and Donald Wells. 8: Photolabs Royal Observatory, Edinburgh. 9: J. A. Hackwell, R. D. Gehrz, and G. L. Grasdalen, courtesy Cerro Tololo Inter-American Observatory, Chile, and The Aerospace Corporation; University of Leicester, X-Ray Astronomy Group/Science Photo Library, London. 10: Official Naval Observatory Photograph. 11: National Radio Astronomy Observatory—Ralph Bolin and Ted Stecher/Science Photo Library, London; this near-infrared image of M51 was taken at the 48-inch Schmidt telescope on Mount Palomar by Debra Elmegreen, and has been processed at the IBM T. J. Watson Research Center by Debra and Bruce Elmegreen and Philip Seiden. 12: Dr. Roger Lynds/National Optical Astronomy Observatories, 1974. 13: University of Manchester/Jodrell Bank; NASA. 14-17: Art by Stephen R. Wagner. 18: Courtesy of the Department of Archives and Records Management, Corning Glass Works, Corning, N.Y. 20, 21: Art by Douglas R. Chezem. 22: Art by Stephen R. Wagner. 24, 25: Art by Tina Taylor. 26, 27: Art by Matt McMullen. 28-31: Art by Stephen R. Wagner. 33: John Walsh/Photo Researchers, Inc.—J. Anthony Tyson from AT&T Bell Laboratories and Pat Seitzer from Cerro Tololo Inter-American Observatory, Chile. 34, 35: Art by Steve Bauer from Bill Burrows Studio. 37: Art by Stephen R. Wagner. 39-41: Art by Al Kettler. 43-48: Art by Jeffrey Oh. 49: Art by Tina Taylor. 50, 51: Art by Jeffrey Oh. 52, 53: Art by Stephen R. Wagner. 54: Courtesy of AT&T Archives. 56: The National Radio Astronomy Observatory, operated by Associated Universities, Inc., under contract with the National Science Foundation. 59: The National Radio Astronomy Observatory, operated by Associated Universities, Inc., under contract with the National Science Foundation. 60: Art by Stephen R. Wagner. 62: The National Radio Astronomy Observatory, operated by Associated Universities, Inc., under contract with the National Science Foundation. Observers: Richard A. Perley and John W. Dreher. 63: The National Radio Astronomy Observatory, operated by Associated Universities, Inc., under contract with the National Science Foundation. Observers: Richard A. Perley, John W. Dreher, and John J. Cowen. 64, 65: Art by Alvin Pagan. 67: Art by Stephen R. Wagner. 69: NASA. 71: Art by John Drummond. 72: NASA. 75: Art by Lilli Robbins. 76, 77: Art by Lilli Robbins, except photograph lower left, E. B. Fomalont, P. Parma, R. D. Ekers, and C. Lari. 78, 79: Art by Lilli Robbins, except photograph lower left, E. B. Fomalont, P. Parma, R. D. Ekers, and C. Lari. 80, 81: Art by Lilli Robbins—photograph, E. B. Fomalont, P. Parma, R. D. Ekers, and C. Lari; Art by Lilli Robbins; design configurations, Napier, Thompson, and Ekers (1983), *Journal of Proceedings of IEEE,* Vol. 71, pp. 1295-1320. 82, 83: Art by Lilli Robbins, except photograph left, E. B. Fomalont, P. Parma, R. D. Ekers, and C. Lari. 84-89: Art by Stephen R. Wagner. 90-93: Art by Al Kettler. 94-96: Art by Stephen R. Wagner. 99: John Bedke/Space Telescope Science Institute and California Institute of Technology. This material was produced as an account of the U.S. Government under prime contract NAS5-26555 by the California Institute of Technology for the Association of Universities for Research in Astronomy, Inc. (AURA), Space Telescope Science Institute, Baltimore, Maryland, and may not be reproduced, copied, or otherwise distributed without prior written consent of AURA. 100, 101: Art by Al Kettler—John Bedke/Space Telescope Science Institute, Guide Star Catalog Group, Baltimore, Md. 103-106: Art by Stephen R. Wagner. 109: Art by David Jonason/The Pushpin Group. 110: M. Seldner, B. Siebers, E. J. Groth, and P. J. E. Peebles, 1977, *Astronomical Journal,* 82, p. 249, inset art by David Jonason/The Pushpin Group. 111-117: Art by David Jonason/The Pushpin Group. 118, 119: M. Seldner, B. Siebers, E. J., Groth, and P. J. E. Peebles, 1977, *Astronomical Journal,* 82, p. 249; art by David Jonason/The Pushpin Group.

Acknowledgments

The editors wish to thank the following individuals and institutions for their help: **In Canada:** Calgary—Michael R. Williams; **In France:** Paris—Jacqueline Lamonie, European Space Agency; René Oosterlink, Chef de la Gestion du Personnel, European Space Agency; **In the United States:** Arizona—Amado: Daniel Brocious and Carol Heller, Whipple Observatory; Mesa: Russell M. Genet, Fairborn Observatory; Tucson: Michael G. M. Cawson, Frederic H. Chaffee, Jr., Keith Hege, Jan McCoy, John McGraw, Anthony Poyner, Robert R. Shannon, and Simon D. M. White, University of Arizona; California—Berkeley: John Gustafson, California Association for Research in Astronomy; Pasadena: Tom Chester, James Janesick, Gerry Smith, and James Westphal, California Institute of Technology; Gerry Levy, Ed Olson, Aden B. Meinel, and Mary Beth Murrill, Jet Propulsion Laboratory; Connecticut—Danbury: Terry Facey, Perkin-Elmer Corporation; District of Columbia: Jane Gruenebaum; J. C. Hood, Robert V. Stachnik, National Aeronautics & Space Agency; Georgia—Atlanta: Bill Bagnuolo, Georgia State University; Illinois—Urbana: Ronald J. Allen, University of Illinois; Kansas—Lawrence: Adrian L. Melott, University of Kansas; Maryland—Baltimore: Riccardo Giacconi, Vicki Ladler, Ethan J. Schreier, Caroline Simpson, and Raymond Villard, Space Telescope Science Institute; Greenbelt: Daniel Y. Gezari and Dave Skillman, Goddard Space Flight Center; Massachusetts—Cambridge: Fred L. Whipple, Smithsonian Astrophysics Observatory; Marblehead: Thomas E. Hoffman, Hoffman Design and Development; New Jersey—Murray Hill: J. Anthony Tyson, AT&T Bell Labs; Princeton: P. J. E. Peebles and Martin Schwarzschild, Princeton University; New Mexico—Socorro: Ron Ekers, National Radio Astronomy Observatory; Pennsylvania—Philadelphia: Joan M. Centrella, Drexel University; Virginia—Arlington: Herbert Friedman; Charlottesville: Robert Havlen, Margaret B. Weems, and Donald C. Wells, National Radio Astronomy Observatory.

Index

Time-Life Books Inc.
is a wholly owned subsidiary of
TIME INCORPORATED

FOUNDER: Henry R. Luce 1898-1967

Editor-in-Chief: Jason McManus
Chairman and Chief Executive Officer:
J. Richard Munro
President and Chief Operating Officer:
N. J. Nicholas, Jr.
Editorial Director: Ray Cave
Executive Vice President, Books: Kelso F. Sutton
Vice President, Books: George Artandi

TIME-LIFE BOOKS INC.

EDITOR: George Constable
Executive Editor: Ellen Phillips
Director of Design: Louis Klein
Director of Editorial Resources: Phyllis K. Wise
Editorial Board: Russell B. Adams, Jr.,
Dale M. Brown, Roberta Conlan, Thomas H.
Flaherty, Lee Hassig, Donia Ann Steele,
Rosalind Stubenberg, Henry Woodhead
Director of Photography and Research:
John Conrad Weiser
Assistant Director of Editorial Resources:
Elise Ritter Gibson

PRESIDENT: Christopher T. Linen
Chief Operating Officer: John M. Fahey, Jr.
Senior Vice Presidents: Robert M. DeSena,
James L. Mercer, Paul R. Stewart
Vice Presidents: Stephen L. Bair, Ralph J. Cuomo,
Neal Goff, Stephen L. Goldstein, Juanita T. James,
Hallett Johnson III, Carol Kaplan, Susan J. Maruyama,
Robert H. Smith, Joseph J. Ward
Director of Production Services: Robert J. Passantino

Editorial Operations
Copy Chief: Diane Ullius
Production: Celia Beattie
Library: Louise D. Forstall

Correspondents: Elisabeth Kraemer-Singh (Bonn);
Maria Vincenza Aloisi, (Paris); Ann Natanson (Rome);
Dick Berry (Tokyo). Valuable assistance was also pro-
vided by: Elizabeth Brown and Christina Lieberman
(New York).

UNDERSTANDING COMPUTERS

SERIES DIRECTOR: Lee Hassig
Series Administrator: Loretta Britten

Editorial Staff for *Computers and the Cosmos*
Designer: Robert K. Herndon
Associate Editors: Susan V. Kelly (pictures),
Robert A. Doyle (text)
Researchers: Katya Sharpe Cooke, Edward O.
Marshall, Pamela L. Whitney
Writer: Robert M. S. Somerville
Assistant Designer: Sue Deal-Daniels
Copy Coordinator: Elizabeth Graham
Picture Coordinators: Renée DeSandies, Robert H.
Wooldridge, Jr.
Editorial Assistant: Susan L. Finken

Special Contributors: Joseph Alper, Ronald H. Bailey,
Marcia Bartusiak, Elisabeth Carpenter, Ron Cowen,
Bonnie Gordon, Susan V. Lawrence, Ann Miller,
Charles Smith, Brooke C. Stoddard, Wallace Tucker
(text); Roxie France-Nuriddin, Julie A. Trudeau, Hattie
A. Wicks (research); Mel Ingber (index)

THE CONSULTANTS

RAYMOND CARLBERG is a faculty member in the Department of Astronomy at the University of Toronto. He
has published papers on spiral waves and the cosmological dynamics of galaxy formation and clustering.

CRAIG FOLTZ, a staff astronomer at the Multiple Mirror
Telescope Observatory, holds a Ph. D. in astronomy from
the Ohio State University. His research interests include
the observational study of active galactic nuclei as well
as astronomical instrumentation.

EDWARD B. FOMALONT, an astronomer at the National
Radio Astronomy Observatory, was project manager for
the Astronomical Image Processing System (AIPS), which
is used extensively worldwide to produce and process
radio astronomy images.

SANJOY GHOSH is a space physicist at the NASA Goddard Space Flight Center, where he does computer modeling of magnetized fluids.

CLINTON JANES, the assistant director for Engineering at
the Multiple Mirror Telescope Observatory, was an electronics engineer at McDonald Observatory, Kitt Peak
National Observatory, and Cerro Tololo Interamerican
Observatory, before accepting his present assignment in
1983.

HAROLD A. MCALISTER is an astronomy and physics
professor at Georgia State University and director of the
Center for High Angular Resolution Astronomy. He is a
leading practitioner of speckle interferometry.

IAN S. MCLEAN is a principal scientific officer at the Joint
Astronomy Center of the United Kingdom, Canada, and
the Netherlands located in Hilo, Hawaii. He is currently
writing a book on the history of the CCD.

Library of Congress Cataloging in Publication Data

Computers and the cosmos/by the editors of Time-Life Books.
  p.   cm.—(Understanding computers)
  Bibliography: p.
  Includes index.
  1. Astronomy—Data processing.   2. Astrophysics—Data
processing.   3. Cosmology—Data processing.   4. Life
on other planets—Data processing.   I. Time-Life Books.
II. Series.
QB51 .3.E43C65 1988   520' .28.5—dc19   88-12239
                                                            CIP

ISBN 0-8094-5729-6
ISBN 0-8094-5730-X (lib. bdg.)

For information on and a full description of any of the Time-
Life Books series listed, please write:
Reader Information
Time-Life Customer Service
P.O. Box C-32068
Richmond, Virginia 23261-2068